Constitutional Law in Sweden

Constitutional Law in Sweden

Second Edition

Joakim Nergelius

This book was originally published as a monograph in the International Encyclopaedia of Laws/Constitutional Law.

General Editors: Roger Blanpain, Frank Hendrickx
Volume Editors: André Alen, David Haljan

Wolters Kluwer
Law & Business

Published by:
Kluwer Law International
PO Box 316
2400 AH Alphen aan den Rijn
The Netherlands
Website: www.kluwerlaw.com

Sold and distributed in North, Central and South America by:
Aspen Publishers, Inc.
7201 McKinney Circle
Frederick, MD 21704
United States of America
Email: customer.service@aspenpublishers.com

Sold and distributed in all other countries by:
Turpin Distribution Services Ltd.
Stratton Business Park
Pegasus Drive, Biggleswade
Bedfordshire SG18 8TQ
United Kingdom
Email: kluwerlaw@turpin-distribution.com

Printed on acid-free paper.

ISBN 978-90-411-5880-2

This title is available on www.kluwerlawonline.com

Printed and Bound by CPI Group (UK) Ltd, Croydon, CR0 4YY.

FSC
MIX
FSC® C103993

The Author

Joakim Nergelius is Professor of law at the University of Örebro, Sweden, since September 2003, as well as associate professor (docent) in European and Comparative Law at Abo Academy (Turku), Finland. He has written extensively on Swedish, comparative and European constitutional law. Among his works are *Konstitutionellt rättighetsskydd – Svensk rätt i ett komparativt perspektiv* (Constitutional Protection of Human Rights – Swedish Law in a Comparative Perspective), *Stockholm (Norstedts)* 1996 (doctoral dissertation). *Amsterdamfördraget och EU:s institutionella maktbalans* (The Treaty of Amsterdam and the Institutional Power Balance in the EU), *Stockholm (Norstedts; Institutet för rättsvetenskaplig forskning)* 1998, and the anthology *Nordic and Other European Constitutional Traditions, Brill/Nijhoff* (Leiden/Boston) 2006. More recently, he published the book *The Constitutional Dilemma of the European Union* in 2009 and *The Monography Svensk Statsrätt* (3rd ed. 2014).

The Author

Table of Contents

The Author 3

List of Abbreviations 9

Preface 11

General Introduction 13

Chapter 1. Concise Description of Constitutional History 14

Chapter 2. Profile of the Form of Government 17

Chapter 3. State Territory and Other Geographical and Demographic Data 19

Part I. Sources of Constitutional Law (Notion, Concepts and Hierarchy) 21

§1. INTRODUCTION 21

Chapter 1. Treaties 22

Chapter 2. Constitution 24

Chapter 3. Legislation and Equivalent Legislative Rules 26

Chapter 4. Administrative Regulations and Orders. Regulations and Decrees 27

Chapter 5. Other Sources of Law 31

Part II. Form of Government 33

Chapter 1. General 33

§1. Introduction: Central Authorities of the State 33

§2. Political Parties, Lobbies and Interest Groups 35

§3. Referendum as an Alternative to Representative Democracy 39

Chapter 2. Head of State 41

Chapter 3. The Legislature 45

§1. The Organ of State 45

§2. Legal Status 47

§3. Competences 49
I. Legislation: Further on Chapter 8 of the Instrument of Government 49
II. Budgetary and Financial Power: Instrument of Government Chapter 9 51

§4. Delegation and Distribution of Legislative Power: Relation to the European Union 54
I. Background and General Remarks 54
II. The European Issue in Chapter 10 of the Instrument of Government 57
III. The EMU Issue 64
IV. Conclusions 66

§5. Working Procedures of the Parliament Concerning Legislation 68

Chapter 4. The Executive 72

§1. The Organ of State: Its Legal Status, Competences and Working Modes 72

§2. Governmental Accountability in Relation to Parliament 78

§3. Governmental Accountability in Relation to Public Authorities 84

Chapter 5. The Judiciary and the Independence of the Courts 89

§1. JUDICIAL ORGANIZATION 89

§2. LEGAL STATUS OF THE JUDGES 90

Part III. The State and Its Subdivisions 93

§1. DISTRIBUTION OF POWERS BETWEEN THE STATE AND THE MUNICIPALITIES 93

§2. THE REGIONAL ISSUE 96

Part IV. Human Rights and Judicial Review 99

Chapter 1. Human Rights in Sweden 99

§1. GENERAL REMARKS 99

§2. THE CATALOGUE OF HUMAN RIGHTS IN CHAPTER 2 OF THE INSTRUMENT OF GOVERNMENT 104
I. Background and Structure 104
II. The Individual Rights 105
III. The Range and Extent of the Rights 109

§3. THE FREEDOM OF PRESS ACT 111

§4. THE FREEDOM OF SPEECH ACT 115

Chapter 2. Judicial Review in Swedish Law 117

§1. RELATION BETWEEN JUDICIAL REVIEW AND JUDICIAL PREVIEW 117

§2. THE DEVELOPMENT OF JUDICIAL REVIEW: A BRIEF HISTORICAL BACKGROUND 119

§3. SOME IMPORTANT CASES 122

§4. JUDICIAL REVIEW IN RELATION TO EUROPEAN LAW 124
I. Introduction 124
II. Two Unexpected Judgments from 2005 129
III. Conclusions and a View to the Future 136

Part V. Specific Problems 137

§1. War Powers 137

§2. Emergency Laws 138

§3. The Constitutional Relationship between Church and State 139

Selected Bibliography 141

Index 143

List of Abbreviations

AD	Arbetsdomstolen (Labour Court)
BVerfG	Bundesverfassungsgericht, German Constitutional Court
Ds	Departementsserien
ECHR	European Convention of Human Rights
ECJ	European Court of Justice
ECR	European Court Reports
ECtHR	European Court of Human Rights
EEA	European Economic Area
ERT	Europarättslig tidskrift (European Law Journal)
FPA	Freedom of Press Act, Tryckfrihetsförordningen (1949)
FSA	Freedom of Speech Act, Yttrandefrihetsgrundlagen (1991)
IG	The Instrument of Government, Regeringsformen
KU	Konstitutionsutskottet
MP	Member of Parliament
NJA	Nytt Juridiskt Arkiv
PM	Prime Minister
Prop	Proposition (law bill)
RÅ	Regeringsrättens Årsbok
SEK	Swedish Crowns, official currency
SNS	Studieförbundet Näringsliv och Samhälle
SOU	Statens offentliga utredningar
U	Ugeskrift for Retsvaesen, Danish Case Collection

Preface

It is a great honour and pleasure for me to be able to publish a volume on Swedish Constitutional Law in the well-known series International Encyclopaedia of Laws (Constitutional Laws). As such, this volume is undoubtedly one of the first profound studies in English of the Swedish Constitution. I believe that it comes at an interesting and appropriate time, when the traditionally dominating principles of popular sovereignty and parliamentarianism are becoming ever more challenged by new influences from European law and when the scope of judicial review is in fact growing very clearly.

Traditionally, Sweden has in the twentieth century lived in a kind of peaceful bubble, developing peacefully, in harmony and stability, staying outside both World Wars, establishing democracy early and gradually also developing a generally admired welfare state. This peaceful history did also affect the framing of the new Constitution of 1974, which undoubtedly displays a high degree of trust and belief from the public in the work of the politicians. The point of departure, then, was definitely not the need to protect the individual from the state, but rather to make the state strong in order for it to be able to help the individuals achieve as good a life as possible. Gradually, however, in Sweden like in other states, this general belief in the wholly good force of political work, which leads for instance to almost unrestricted powers for the legislators, has come to be severely questioned and criticized.

In a way, that tension is at the moment the most crucial one in order to understand the current Swedish constitutional debate, in particular since a huge constitutional reform took place in 2010. However, also other interesting features need to be observed and analysed: for instance, how can Sweden, that has almost always been led by Social Democrats, still be a monarchy? And how does the well-known autonomy and independence of the public organs work in practice? What are the results of the incorporation of the European Convention on Human Rights into Swedish law? And how is regional or, more importantly, municipal autonomy affected by EU membership?

Hopefully, the interested reader may here find the answer to these and other relevant questions. The text book can then hopefully also contribute to a better understanding of the Swedish society, at least seen from its more formal aspects.

One of the main aims of this book, thus, is to explain and present those new constitutional rules, that in particular will enforce the rule of the courts, make it more difficult for 'sitting' governments to remain in power after the elections and clarify certain items concerning the autonomy of the municipalities. Since this is a major constitutional reform, on which the political parties and numerous experts have been working a long time, the constitution does not look likely to change in a long time after that. But then again, who knows what might happen?

Örebro, September 2014
Joakim Nergelius

General Introduction

Type of government:	Parliamentary democracy
Type of state:	Unitary state
Type of legislature:	Unicameral parliament
Date of constitution:	1 January 1975. Three other Constitutional Acts, from 1810, 1949 and 1991 respectively, do, however, also exist.
Date of last amendment:	27 November 2010

Chapter 1. Concise Description of Constitutional History

1. The most important of the constitutional acts, Regeringsformen (The Instrument of Government), was enacted in 1974 and entered into force in 1975. Additionally, the 1810 Act of Succession, regulating the succession to the throne, and the 1949 Freedom of Press Act (which traces its origins back to 1766) are both important parts of the Swedish constitutional heritage, whereas the Freedom of Speech Act from 1991 is an extension of the latter one, making it applicable also to new media such as TV and movies.

2. A number of important basic human rights are covered both by the Instrument of Government and by the European Convention of Human Rights, which has been applied as domestic Swedish law since 1995. However, in general, the constitutional tradition in Sweden is weak, and it is only in the last ten years that an increased interest in constitutional issues has become visible among scholars and the media.

3. The first written Swedish constitution dates back to the fourteenth century, the so-called *Konungabalken* (King's Act) of what is referred to as *Magnus Eriksson's landslag* (national law). The Act contained rules on how to elect kings and high officials and on the tasks of the Council (*råd*), the government of the time.

4. Despite a few modifications, this basic 'constitution' continued to apply at least in part until 1634, when the first Instrument of Government or *Regeringsform* was enacted. (The birth of the modern Swedish state in 1523 did thus not alter the constitutional development as such.) The Instrument of Government was a very modern constitution for its time; it established the administrative features of the Swedish state that still largely exist. Because of the centralization of the administration, the main public authorities were regulated in the constitution. The relative strength of the administrative tradition compared with the constitutional tradition can be, in part, traced to this period.

5. It was under this constitution that an embryonic parliamentarism was developed for the first time. It was decided in 1660 that the four social classes (*stånd, ständer*) – aristocracy, clergy, merchants and farmers – should form a parliament. This was the basis for Swedish parliamentarism until 1866, when a bicameral system was introduced. Nevertheless, autocracy prevailed for some time.

6. The next Instrument of Government, in 1720, emphasized the different functions of the state in a clearer way, and it was under this modernized constitution that political parties came into existence. The king had to govern the country according to the wishes of the Council; he himself had two votes, but he had to bow to the will of the majority. It was also during this period that the concept of a constitutional law – more difficult to change than an ordinary law – took hold, and it became necessary to define which laws that were constitutional. One of those so defined was the 1766 Freedom of Press Act, containing, among other things, rules on public access to documents. It was also in 1766 that the well-known institution of the *Ombudsman* originally was founded.

7. After yet another period of autocracy, the king had to resign in 1809, and a new constitution was established. This 1809 Instrument of Government formally remained in force until the end of 1974, by which time it had become the second oldest written constitution in use anywhere in the world. This fact illustrates the peaceful development that the country has enjoyed for the last two centuries. However, some of the most important provisions in the 1809 constitution, such as the right of the king to govern the state alone, or his two votes in the highest court, gradually became obsolete. After the general democratic breakthrough of the early 1920s, most of the constitution was seen to have lost force and validity.

8. There were a number of reasons why the Constitution of 1809 so quickly lost its influence, of which the introduction of the bicameral Parliament in 1866 is one. The democratization around 1920 also made its provisions concerning e.g., the power of the king obsolete. After that, crucial constitutional events like legislation, appointment of the government et cetera took place in a way that was not in accordance with the formal constitution, which is definitely one of the main reasons why the Swedish constitutional tradition is so weak compared to many other democratic states.[1] The peaceful domestic development is undoubtedly another one.

9. Under the 1809 constitution, the executive power belonged to the king, and the legislative power was divided between parliament and king; up until a court reform in 1909, the king also held some judicial powers. A new Freedom of Press Act was introduced in 1810 and 1812, as well as a new Parliamentary Regulation or Riksdag Act (*Riksdagsordningen*). That same year, the current Act of Succession was introduced; the same royal family (Bernadotte, of French origin) has held the throne ever since.

10. A new wave of constitutional reform nevertheless began to be prepared in the 1950s, when the situation without a formal constitution was being seen as somewhat a problem, after all. The bicameral parliament was replaced by a one-chamber system in 1970, and the current constitution was enacted in 1974. Significant reforms were added in 1976, 1979, and 1994, in particular strengthening the protection of basic human rights. Nevertheless, the emphasis on popular sovereignty is still very strong. A core concept of the constitution is that all political power rests with parliament, representing the people. Here, it would seem that the few elements of separation of powers that occurred in the 1809 constitution, in combination with the fact that the development in the Swedish society was generally positive after 1920, when the emphasis was instead put on popular sovereignty, had led to general political unanimity on the need to let popular sovereignty prevail in the new constitution. It should also be noted that this was enacted in 1974, when the Swedish

1. One author, Fredrik Sterzel, has described the period from 1920–1974 as 'the half-century without a constitution', which seems to be a good description. See in particular his book Författning i utveckling, Uppsala 1998 for further details.

welfare state had reached its peak in terms of success and the general, deep belief in the wisdom of politicians and their decision-making was thus widespread. Now, in 2010, an element of separation of powers has finally been introduced in the constitution, with a whole new rule for the courts.

11. In this constitution, the monarchy has remained, but the king has been stripped of all formal powers, left with only purely representative functions. A distinctive political feature has of course been the fact that one political party, the Social Democrats, has been very dominant, holding political power from 1932–1976, 1982–1991 and 1994–2006 (and again since October 2014). Still, Sweden has to a surprisingly high extent avoided corruption and similar problems that are normally related to an absence of change in political power, which can most likely be explained by the high degree of transparency within the public administration.

12. From a general point of view, the most important constitutional change since 1974 is undoubtedly the accession to the European Union (EU) on 1 January 1995. The traditionally strong legislature suddenly lost some of its power, having to share its sovereignty with a *supra*-national legislator. The incorporation of the European Convention on Human Rights into Swedish national law also contributed to a generally increased interest in constitutional issues.

Chapter 2. Profile of the Form of Government

13. Sweden is a parliamentary democracy based on popular sovereignty and the rule of law. The independence of the executive, legislative and judicial powers is guaranteed through various provisions of the constitution, even though the principle of separation of powers was clearly not a core value when the constitution was promulgated in the 1960s and 1970s. The political atmosphere in Sweden and the other Nordic countries was permeated with the idea of popular sovereignty, which was seen as the ideological basis of the successful welfare state. Later, in particular after 1 January 1995 when Sweden joined the EU, the idea of separation of powers became more influential.

14. The parliament (Riksdag, riksdagen) consists of 349 members, sitting in one-chamber. National elections take place every fourth year in September; elections for the 285 municipalities take place at the same time. The election system is strictly proportional. Each party that wins at least 4% of the votes in the country is represented in parliament.

Sweden is still a monarchy, although the tasks of the king are mainly representative. Political power rests with the parliament and, in particular, with the executive branch of the government. Within the executive, the prime minister has a very strong position.

15. As mentioned above, the most important of the constitutional acts, Regeringsformen (The Instrument of Government), was enacted in 1974 and entered into force in 1975. Additionally, both the 1810 Act of Succession, regulating the succession to the throne, and the 1949 Freedom of Press Act (which traces its origins back to 1766), as well as the new Freedom of Speech Act from 1991, which regulates the freedom of speech in other media than books and journals, are both important parts of the Swedish constitutional heritage. Furthermore, a number of important basic human rights are covered both by the Instrument of Government and by the European Convention of Human Rights, which has applied as domestic Swedish law since 1995.

16. In the Instrument of Government, the basic principles of the form of government are to be found in Chapter 1. Those include popular sovereignty in Article 1,[2] which states that all public power in Sweden proceeds from the people and that Swedish democracy, which is founded on the free formation of opinion and on universal and equal suffrage, shall be realized through a representative and parliamentary polity and through local self-government. It also mentions that public power shall be exercised under the law; according to Article 2, public power shall be exercised with respect for the equal worth for all and the liberty and dignity of the private person. In section 2, that Article also makes note of social, economic and cultural rights, as well as environmental and other rights, though those rights are in fact not legally protected as such by the constitution or by the Swedish legal order,

2. As well as Art. 4, which underlines the supreme position of the Parliament.

which may be slightly surprising for many guest scholars and other visitors or students of the Swedish welfare system. Instead, Chapter 1, Article 2 IG is a pure statement on the aims and purposes of the public sector and the public activity in general, including a duty for public authorities to combat discrimination of persons.

17. Article 3 enumerates the constitutional acts, while Articles 5–6 mention the Monarchy and the Government respectively, without adding any substantial new information to what is generally known concerning the function of those bodies. The same could be said concerning Article 8 on courts and other public (national or local) authorities, as well as Article 7 on municipalities and county councils, which is however legally interesting through the statement in its section 2 that the local authorities may levy taxes in order to perform their tasks, the content and significance of which has been subject to vivid discussions.[3] It suffices here to say that this last statement seems to be legally more precise than most other rules within this general, introductory and very principled Chapter.

18. The same could be said for Chapter 1, Article 9, according to which courts of law, administrative authorities and others performing tasks within the public administration shall have regard in their work to the equality of all before the law and shall thus observe objectivity and impartiality. Clear violations of this so-called objectivity rule could be subject to actions before a court. The same is likely to be true concerning Chapter 1, Article 7, section 2, though the issue is very contested, but not in relation to the other parts of Chapter 1.

Finally, after the changes in 2010, a new rule in Chapter 1, Article 10 states that Sweden is a member of the EU and that Sweden also participates in various forms of international cooperation through the UN, the Council of Europe and other channels.

3. This question will be dealt with further below in Part III, Ch. 2.

Chapter 3. State Territory and Other Geographical and Demographic Data

Capital:	Stockholm
Population:	9,639,741 (2013 est.)
Size:	173,732 sq mi (449.963 sq km). Besides France and Spain, Sweden is thus the largest Member State of the EU.
Languages:	Swedish. Four languages have official status as a minority language, Finnish, Hebrew, Sami, and a dialect of Finnish spoken in the border region in the far north between Sweden and Finland
Religion:	Protestant 87%, other (Roman Catholic, Orthodox, Baptist, Muslim, Jewish, Buddhist) 13%
National or ethnic composition:	Swedish 80%, immigrants of different origins 20%
Date of independence or creation:	6 June 1523

Part I. Sources of Constitutional Law (Notion, Concepts and Hierarchy)

§1. Introduction

19. The Swedish legal system is based, like most other legal systems in the world, on the idea of an existing hierarchy of norms. Still, that is not very clearly expressed in the Swedish constitution, where it may only indirectly be deduced from the role on judicial review in Chapter 11, Article 14 of the IG, according to which courts or other public bodies may set aside provisions that are in conflict with rules of fundamental law 'or other superior statute'.

20. This provision, though rarely used, would of course be meaningless without an existing hierarchy of norms. Nevertheless, that concept has in fact never been very clearly developed in Swedish constitutional law, where it may even be said that the concept of the Constitution as *higher law* or *lex superior* was not very clear when the Instrument of Government (which is by far the most important constitutional act) was adapted in 1974. At that time, a perspective highly inspired by popular sovereignty prevailed, according to which the constitution contains rules that describe the political situation and for instance what should happen and which procedure that is to be followed when the PM is appointed or laws are enacted and in similar situations or, in other words, that the Constitution is above all *descriptive*. The opposite and internationally more common view, based on constitutionalism, according to which the Constitution is the *higher law*, against which all other laws are to be measured and reviewed, has only quite recently, in the last ten years and in the light of the wholly new influence of European law, started to be discussed. Undoubtedly, that new perspective is now gaining ground, which could be seen not least in the official, governmental instructions (2004:96) to the Parliamentary committee preparing a constitutional reform for 2010 (*Grundlagsutredningen*).[4]

4. In the doctrine, this tension between old and new ideas and perspectives, between popular sovereignty and constitutionalism in other words, is analysed in particular by Nergelius, Svensk statsrätt, in Ch. 1 and in the structure of the book, which is built around this distinction.

Chapter 1. Treaties

21. Treaties entered into by Sweden do not form part of the Swedish constitution, and are in fact not even part of Swedish law at all until they have been incorporated or transformed into Swedish national law. In other words, Sweden traditionally has a dualistic view on the relationship between national and international law.[5]

22. This may be illustrated by the fate of the European Convention of Human Rights (ECHR) in Swedish law. Sweden ratified this convention already in 1951 (although the jurisdiction of the European Court of Human Rights was not acknowledged until 1966), but it was not incorporated into Swedish national law until 1995, when Sweden joined the EU. Thus, for forty-five years, the Convention was never a part of Swedish law and could strictly speaking not be invoked in proceedings before Swedish national courts, though its great practical importance meant that it was nevertheless used by high Swedish courts and in particular the Supreme Court as a means of interpretation, in particular in the late 1980s and early 1990s, after Sweden had been condemned for violations in a number of cases before the Strasbourg court. This meant that this particular convention came to have a certain or even considerable importance in Swedish law before even being incorporated, but that is a clear exception from the main, general rule.

23. In relation to treaties and international law in general, the more detailed rules concerning the EU are dealt with below in Part II Chapter 3, since they are extremely important in relation to the legislative power. Concerning other treaties or other forms of international cooperation, the provision in Chapter 10, Article 7, section 1 must be observed, which states that a right of decision-making which is based on the IG and consists either in legislation, the use of the assets of the State or the conclusion or denunciation of an international agreement or obligation, may to a limited extent be transferred to an international organization for peaceful cooperation of which Sweden is a member, or is about to become a member, or to an international court. Such transfer, which shall take place in the same way as a constitutional amendment or by means of a decision in which at least five sixths of those voting and three-fourths of the total number of MP's (i.e., 262) concur, may however not relate to matters concerning constitutional enactment, amendment or abrogation or to restriction of any constitutionally protected fundamental rights. Those requirements are considerably harsher and more severe than the ones that pertain to transfer of similar competences to the European Commission (EU), which is thus after all in a somewhat 'privileged position' here.[6]

---

5. See on this topic most recently Vilhelm Persson, Rättsliga ramar för gränsöverskridande samarbete – Förvaltningsmyndigheters internationella avtalsförhållanden, Lund 2005, p. 203 f.
6. Also the two last ss 2–3 of Ch. 10, Art. 7 and Art. 9 may be mentioned here. According to Art. 9, the Parliament may prescribe, once it has been laid down in law that an international agreement shall have validity as Swedish law, that also future amendments of the agreement in question shall be binding for Sweden (with the same kind of majority that was envisaged in s. 2). And according to the practically more important Art. 8, any judicial or administrative function which is not directly based on the IG may be transferred, except to the EU, to another state, international organization or foreign or

24. Agreements with other states or international agreements are concluded by the Government under Chapter 10, Article 1, which is logical given that the Government does after all govern the Realm according to Chapter 1, Article 6 IG, as mentioned in the introduction. All agreements that pre-suppose the amendment or abrogation of an act of law or the enactment of a new act of law, or concerns any other area of the Parliament's competence, must however be approved by the Parliament, as follows from Chapter 10, Article 3. For smaller, more uncomplicated agreements that do not require the participation of the Parliament,[7] the Government may under Chapter 10, Article 2 even commission an administrative authority to conclude them.

---

international institution or community by means of a decision of the Parliament, who may also in law authorize the Government or another public authority to approve such a transfer of functions in particular cases. If this function should involve the exercise of public authority (*myndighetsutövning*) a qualified majority procedure will apply, but otherwise not.

7. Or of the special Advisory Committee on Foreign Affairs, consisting of the Speaker and nine other MP's but presided by the King (!), which is regulated more in detail in Ch. 10, Arts 11–12.

Chapter 2. Constitution

25. Constitutional law is by tradition that part of law which studies the constitution(s). In Sweden, this means that no less than four Constitutional Acts are studied; that is, apart from the important Instrument of Government (*Regeringsformen*) from 1974, also the Act of Succession (*Successionsordningen*) from 1810, which regulates the right to the throne, as well as the Freedom of Press Act (Tryckfrihetsförordningen) from 1949 and the Freedom of Speech Act (*Yttrandefrihetsgrundlagen*) from 1991, which both regulate the freedom of speech as a human right, the first one in books and journals and the latter, new one in other media (those acts will be further dealt with below in Part IV). At the same time, however, constitutional law in Sweden as in other countries also include the study of a number of ordinary laws and other inferior rules which are of importance in this context. The Riksdag Act is by far the most important one of those rules, but also a number of other, ordinary laws do of course matter here.

26. Once again, the main trait or characteristic feature of the Swedish Constitution, identified here as IG, is its emphasis on popular sovereignty. According to its very first sentence, in Chapter 1, Article 1, section 1, 'All public power in Sweden proceeds from the people'. This, on the other hand, is not only a declaratory statement against the concept of separation of powers, but a viewpoint and an attitude that influences also other parts of the Swedish constitutional system.

27. One aspect of this principled approach, though perhaps not the most important one, is the relative ease with which the constitution(s) may be changed. According to Chapter 8, Article 14, the constitutional acts or fundamental laws are enacted, changed or amended by means of two decisions of identical wording (see also Articles 15 and 18). The second decision, however, may not be taken until elections for the Riksdag have been held and the newly elected Parliament has been convened. At least nine months shall elapse between the time when the matter was first submitted to the Chamber of the Riksdag and the date of the election, unless the Parliamentary Committee on the Constitution (*Konstitutionsutskottet, KU*) grants an exception from that provision by means of a decision supported by five sixths of its members.[8] But it must be noted that on neither of those occasions is any qualified majority of the 349 MP's required; instead, a majority of the MP's present and voting is sufficient both times, which is surprising and maybe even astonishing in an international perspective.

28. A certain protection for parliamentary minorities is provided by Chapter 8, Article 16, which stipulates that a referendum shall be held on a proposal concerning fundamental law which is held in abeyance over an election, on a motion to this effect by at least one tenth of the MP's, provided that at least one-third of them will

8. In s. 2 of the same article it is also stated that The Riksdag may not adopt as a decision held in abeyance over an election a proposal for the enactment of fundamental law which conflicts with any other proposal concerning fundamental law currently being held in abeyance, unless at the same time it rejects the proposal it first adopted.

concur in approving the motion.[9] The referendum will then be held simultaneously with the parliamentary election. The proposal is rejected if a majority of those taking part in the referendum vote against it and if the number of those voting against it exceeds half the number of those who registered a valid vote in the election.

29. Still, in an international perspective it seems clear that the Swedish constitutional acts are unusually easy to change or amend, in particular when the rules are seen in connection with the fact that the highly technical nature of the Freedom of Press and Speech acts, which both contain huge sections of criminal, procedural and civil law, has led to a series of regular constitutional changes (totally more than 200) since 1974. In fact, for the parliamentary election of September 2006, no proposals for constitutional amendments were proposed, for the first election time since 1974! It should also be noted that the possibility for a referendum on a proposed constitutional amendment, which should in its result be legally and constitutionally binding, has so far never been used.

30. From a political point of view, however, those rules are best understood from the aspect that they contribute to consensus concerning constitutional changes among the main political parties, notably the social democrats and the right-wing parties. In fact, politically disputed or contested constitutional amendments have so far been extremely unusual, which of course in a way has until now diminished the practical importance and consequences of the fact that the Constitutional Acts are so comparatively easy to change or amend.

9. Such a motion must be put forward within fifteen days from the date on which the Riksdag adopted the proposal which is to be held in abeyance.

Chapter 3. Legislation and Equivalent Legislative Rules

31. According to Chapter 1, Article 4, section 1 of the IG, the Riksdag is the foremost representative of the people. It is thus logical, given the emphasis on popular sovereignty that is so characteristic for the Swedish constitution, that legislation is a dominant source of law and that it is easy to pass.

32. The main rule on how legislation is passed is to be found in Chapter 4, Article 7 IG, which states that when a vote is taken in the Riksdag, the opinion in which more than half of those voting concur constitutes the decision of the Riksdag. Legislation is included here, without being expressly mentioned. There are certain rules on requirements for a qualified majority to be found both in the IG and in the Riksdag Act,[10] for various situations, but those are exceptions.

33. Thus, the only 'law' which really deviates from the simple majority rule that is otherwise prevailing in the Swedish constitution is the Riksdag Act, the ordinary provisions of which, according to Chapter 8, Article 17, is enacted either in the same way as the constitutional acts, i.e., through two decisions with an election between them, or by means of one single decision, provided that at least three-fourths of those voting and more than half the total number of MP's will concur. (The same goes for its amendments, Chapter 8, Article 18 section 2.) In other words, this is a good example of minority protection, requiring both qualified and absolute majority, though it relates to the parliamentarians own, internal act, so to speak.[11] For some reason, which may be hard to explain today when Sweden no longer has an official state church, enactment, amendments or changes of any law concerning either the Church of Sweden as a religious community or other religious communities shall also follow the same rules as the Riksdag Act, according to Chapter 8, Article 2 section 4. Otherwise, however, parliamentary supremacy rules totally in this sphere and only a simple majority of MP's are required in order to pass a law.

10. One such example is the transfer of decision-making powers to the European Union, Ch. 10, Art. 5 IG, to be analysed further below in Part II, Ch. 3, s. 3.
11. But only, which should be observed, in relation to its main provisions (*huvudbestämmelser*), not its supplementary provisions (*tilläggsbestämmelser*), which according to Ch. 8, Art. 17 s. 2 are decided in the same way as ordinary laws. – In this respect, it must be noted that according to a proposal from the Parliament itself (*Översyn av Riksdagsordningen*, 2012/12:UR F3), almost all the articles in the Riksdag Act are going to be renumbered as of 1 Sep. 2014, through one single decision, in line with IG Ch. 8, Art. 17. Very few of the rules are however themselves changed.

Chapter 4. Administrative Regulations and Orders. Regulations and Decrees

34. If the rule concerning enactment of laws is fairly simple, the same could definitely not be said about other written rules. Instead, the rules on enactment of regulations, decrees and other rules in Chapter 8 IG are probably the most complicated in all the constitutional acts (together perhaps with some statements in the Freedom of Press and Speech Acts). Also in an international perspective, they appear to be unusually – and unnecessarily – complicated. Still, an attempt to simplify those rules has been made in 2010, in the following way.

35. First of all, it is stated in Chapter 8, Article 2 that the law form is required for a number of different areas, which are to described more in detail below in Part II, Chapter 3.[12] Those rules are quite different to their nature; while sections 1–2 have a great practical importance in terms of determining when legislation is really necessary, sections 3–6 deal with more political issues such as referendas, municipalities and religious communities. After that, then, follow the extremely complicated rules concerning the enactment of regulations and decrees, which are in fact hard to understand also for constitutional experts.

36. The principle underlying those rules, if we may find one, is that the government may be authorized by law – passed by the Parliament – to enact certain rules, if certain conditions are met. At the same time, however, power conferred to the Government to adopt provisions in a particular matter will never preclude the Parliament from adopting provisions in the same matter through an act of law, according to Chapter 8, Article 8. Thus, the Parliament may authorize the Government through law to issue certain rules, then watch this happen and then legislate on the same issue, contrary to the rules that the Government had passed, being authorized to do so by the Parliament in the first place.[13]

37. Still, that is not the strangest rule here, or the most difficult to understand. If we start with Chapter 8, Article 3, which may be seen as a key rule in order to understand the system of the Chapter, it says that with authority in law, the Government may, by means of a statutory instrument adopt provisions relating to matters other than taxes or bankruptcy in a number of areas (in principle those who are mentioned in Article 2 sections 2–3), namely a huge number of areas within administrative law. In none of those cases, however, does this authority confer to the

12. Also certain other rules are important in that respect, like Ch. 11, Art. 2, which regulates procedural law (where only legislation is accepted).
13. Furthermore, any provisions adopted by the Government by virtue of authority in law under IG shall according to Ch. 8, Art. 6 be submitted to the Parliament for examination, should the latter so wish. Thus the Parliament obviously wishes to keep its initiative and authority in the legislative area, for understandable reasons.

government the right to adopt provisions concerning the legal effects of criminal acts, other than the imposition of fines.[14]

38. The idea or method behind this provision, seen together with other parts of Chapter 8, undoubtedly is that certain or in fact big areas of societal life are to be regulated through law, but that deviations are possible within the areas or concerning the issues enumerated in Chapter 8, Article 2 sections 2–3. The other areas, where delegation is thus not possible, is most often referred to as 'the compulsory law area' (*det obligatoriska lagområdet*), while the issues covered by Chapter 8, Article 7 form the 'the area enabling delegation of legislative powers' (*det fakultativa* or *delegeringsbara lagområdet*).

39. That distinction is basic in this context, but also other rules are important here. The most complicated rules are not the ones that also grant the Government the competence with authority in law to adopt, by means of a statutory instrument, provisions concerning the granting of respites for the meeting of obligations (Chapter 8, Article 4). Neither are some more organizational rules in Chapter 8, Article 5, stating that with authority in law the Government may prescribe by means of a statutory interpretation that provisions of certain laws may come into force or cease to apply and Chapter 8, Articles 9–11, according to which the Parliament may, when authorizing the Government to adopt provisions in a particular matter, also authorize the Government to delegate the power to adopt regulations in the matter further below, to an administrative or local authority, very troublesome here.[15] Instead, the two really tricky provisions are Chapter 8, Article 3, section 1 and Article 7, which both need to be further analysed.

40. As follows from Chapter 8, Article 2 as well as Article 3 section 1, and also from Chapter 1, Article 4 IG, the competence to tax or decide on the taxes belongs to the Parliament and may not be delegated.[16] What may be delegated, however, according to Chapter 8, Article 3, section 1 *e contrario*, is the power to decide on fines or charges (without any authority in law required, slightly surprising). The question thus becomes what the difference may be between taxes and charges, where the doctrine has stressed that a tax is paid to the state or to a municipality since that has been duly decided, without any direct compensation being received (except in the indirect form of functioning schools, roads, hospitals et cetera). A charge or fine, on the other hand, is normally related to some kind of favour to be

14. Still, the Parliament may according to the very last sentence of the provision prescribe legal effects other than fines for contraventions of provisions laid down by the Government in a legal act which the latter is authorized to enact under Ch. 8, Art. 3 s. 2 (*former* Art. 7). How this difficult provision is to be interpreted was dealt with by the Supreme Court in a case in 2005, NJA 2005, p. 33, where a provision on prison crime for a certain, minor sentence was actually set aside because it was held to violate *the former* Ch. 8, Art. 7.

15. Whereas the Parliament is probably not, according to dominating opinions in the doctrine, able to delegate powers itself directly to a public authority (see Nergelius, *supra*, p. 90 with further references), with a small exception for authorities residing under the Parliament itself in their own matters, Ch. 8, Art. 13, s. 2.

16. See also Ch. 8, Art. 7, s. 2, 2nd sentence concerning local or municipal taxation, in the area of which that does of course not apply.

obtained from the public sector.[17] Those kind of burdensome charges (*betungande avgifter*) may thus be delegated to the Government or to municipalities to decide upon according to Chapter 8, Articles 2 and 3, section 1. It is obvious that the border between such charges and taxes may sometimes be very hard to distinguish.

41. Apart from what has now been said, there is in fact also a further area, where the Government may enact rules of its own, due to an autonomous competence (so-called *restkompetens*). This area is in Chapter 8, Article 7 partly negatively defined, since it includes provisions which shall *not* under the constitution or fundamental laws be adopted by the Parliament. It also includes provisions relating to the implementation of laws, which is a problematic sector quite of its own since it tends to be very widely defined. Some more precise definitions of what implementation may really mean in this context would have been welcome.

42. The first, negatively defined sector, however, relates to what may be called favourable (*gynnande*) provisions, from the point of view of the individual. Given that the possibility for the Parliament to delegate competence in the area of civil law is very limited (see Chapter 8, Article 2 in relation to Article 3), favourable or beneficial rules in the area of public law will here merit particular attention. The various contributions and transfers from the state is a classical example.

43. It is in fact surprising that those complicated and highly technical rules have not been more contested in the doctrine, given that they seem excessively complicated in order to be included in a constitution and that they have also led to a number of practical difficulties, not least when it comes to distinguishing a certain category of rules from another one. However, in recent years some critical voices have been raised against for instance the unspecified extent of implementation rules that may be used by the Government. The committee preparing a constitutional reform has also signalled a change and a simplification of the rules would quite simply be useful and desirable. A general impression when reading those complicated rules, in Chapter 8, Articles 3–13 in particular, is that they are intended to express a kind of parliamentarism also in this area, in relation to the government, which does in reality no longer exist. The huge expansion of implementation rules and other administrative regulations that has taken place since 1974 means that the rules are, if not obsolete so at least passed by the actual societal development, in particular when combined with the effects of EU membership, which means that the Swedish Parliament has in fact handed over or transferred many legislative and other powers to the EU.[18]

44. Therefore, a reform under which a clear division of legislative and regulative competences between the Parliament and the Government could be introduced, with restricted possibilities to delegate powers, would probably be preferable. The reform in 2010 marks a small step in this direction. The limited difficulties that might after such a move still occur in terms of deciding who is responsible for the

---

17. Cfr Nergelius, *supra*, p. 89.
18. Cfr Nergelius, *supra*, p. 96 ss as well as below in Part II, Ch. 3.

enactment of certain rules could then be left to the courts to decide about, given that the general acceptance of judicial review could increase slightly, which there are now certain signs of. It might also be noted that judicial review is traditionally, anyway, more accepted in this rather technical domain than concerning most other issues.[19]

19. This point will be further illustrated below in Part IV, Ch. 2.

Chapter 5. Other Sources of Law

45. Apart from laws, regulations and other written sources of law that are to be found in the detailed Chapter 8 of IG, other, unwritten sources of law (like General Principles of Law) are traditionally not very important in Swedish law. Some such principles, like the principles of proportionality, objectivity in the public administration and equality before the law, may be found in the text of the IG, but if that is not the case, they are normally not to be reckoned with or taken into account in constitutional interpretation.[20]

46. The same goes for customary law, with one possible exception for what may be called constitutional custom (*konstitutionell praxis*), a term that is however slightly tricky and the significance of which is not really easy to grasp. In terms of jurisprudence, no regular constitutional custom may be said to exist. What has however happened a number of times in particular during the 1990s is that the Government, when proposing new legislation to the Parliament that may actually be unconstitutional or at least doubtful from a constitutional point of view, has referred to the existence of such a thing as a constitutional custom when trying to justify the passing of the new bill into a legal act. In particular, this has been the case in relation to the traditional – but legally undefined – autonomy of the municipalities. The opinions in the doctrine are divided on this point.[21] As a general point of view, this line of reasoning probably has its roots in the period when Sweden lacked a formally and truly binding constitution, i.e., between 1920 and 1974. It seems more strange and even awkward that it will be invoked on a number of occasions now, but this tendency should be seen in the light of the fact that many Swedish politicians and legislators are traditionally unable to recognize and admit the binding, normative force of the Constitution (which is actually one of the main contemporary constitutional problems in Sweden). Thus, it may be an important task for constitutional scholars to protest against such a weak line of reasoning, in particular when it seems to be misused for political purposes.

47. Apart from what has been said here, it should also be noted that so-called *travaux préparatoires* (*lagförarbeten, motiv*) have always been a very important source of law in Sweden, in all areas of law. From a constitutional point of view, this Nordic tradition which is apparently stronger in Sweden than in any other country, could from a constitutional point of view be seen as yet another example of the rather weak position of the courts in relation to the legislator, since it means that the courts have a tradition of following not only the written laws quite literally, but also to pay obedience to the intentions and purposes behind the legislation that the legislator, i.e., a minister, representing the Government, has normally expressed in

---

20. The topic is studied as such in Marcusson, L. (ed.), *Offentligrättsliga principer* (an anthology with Articles on various principles), Uppsala: Iustus 2005. See also A. Peczenik, Principer i det svenska statsskicket, in Berggren/Karlson/Nergelius (eds.), Makt utan motvikt – Om demokrati och konstitutionalism, Stockholm (City University Press) 1999, pp. 109–153.
21. Support has been raised by the retired professor Fredrik Sterzel. For criticism, see Nergelius, *supra*, p. 186.

some motives and bills (normally in the so-called *propositioner*). Still, it is a general assumption that the entry of European law into Swedish national law will gradually lead to a reduced importance for this particular source of law, as compared to before.

Part II. Form of Government

Chapter 1. General

§1. Introduction: Central Authorities of the State

48. Sweden is a parliamentary democracy based on popular sovereignty and rule of law at the same time, as follows from Chapter 1, Article 1 of the Constitution (Instrument of Government) of 1974, which entered into force 1 January 1975. The independence of the respective executive, legislative and judicial powers is guaranteed through various provisions of the Constitution, but the idea of separation of powers was not present when the Constitution, replacing an ancient and partly obsolete Constitution from 1809, was elaborated in the 1960s and 1970s, as mentioned above.

49. The Parliament (Riksdag, riksdagen) consists of 349 members, all sitting in the same chamber. National elections take place every fourth year in September and, at the same time, municipal elections take place to the 285 municipalities. (However, in 2010 the possibility to organize municipal elections between the parliamentary elections was introduced.) The election system is strictly proportional. Each party which gains at least 4% of the votes in the country will be represented in Parliament. At the moment (September 2014), eight parties are represented there.

50. The political power rests with the Parliament and in particular the government. Within the government, the prime minister has a very strong position. In fact, the parliament only votes on his nomination and he is then free to choose any members that he wishes of the government.

51. Sweden has a long history as a highly centralized state, a monarchy with Stockholm as its capital and, since circa 1920, a well-functioning parliamentary democracy. It holds no depending or special territories.

52. As is generally known, Sweden joined the EU together with Finland and Austria on 1 January 1995. The membership found its legal (and political) support in an accession treaty concluded in February 1994 and a referendum on 13 November 1994, in which 52.4% voted yes and 46.7% no. (82% of the registered voters participated in this referendum and it may be noted that only Swedish citizens were allowed to vote, as a contrast to ordinary local elections but in line with parliamentary elections).

53. The major organs of government containing elected officials are the following ones:

PARLIAMENT: The Elections to the Riksdag are regulated in Chapter 3 of the IG. As mentioned already, the Riksdag consists of one single chamber comprising three hundred and forty-nine members. Free secret and direct elections take place every fourth year (previously always on the third Sunday in September, but from 2014 on the second Sunday of September). The votes go to parties, of which seven are currently represented in the Assembly. Every Swedish citizen who has attained the age of eighteen on or before Election Day is entitled to vote. Extraordinary elections for the Riksdag may be called by the government between the ordinary elections, except for the first three months after an ordinary election, but so far this has never happened.
GOVERNMENT: Any description of the position of the Swedish government must be based on a distinction between the prime minister and the other ministers, who are appointed by the prime minister and may also be removed by him at any time (cfr IG Chapter 6, Articles 1 and 8). Thus, after the elections described *above*, or when a prime minister has resigned, a new Prime Minister is to be appointed. The Speaker of the Parliament then summons for consultation representatives from each party group of the Riksdag, before placing a proposal before the Riksdag (which shall vote on the proposal no later than four days afterwards). However, and this is peculiar, the rule in this situation is that if more than half of the Members of the Riksdag (i.e. 175) vote against the proposal it is rejected, whereas in any other case it is adopted. A historical record was here set in 1978, when Mr Ola Ullsten was accepted as prime minister, leading a one-party liberal government, with only 38 votes in favour of him! Still, should the Riksdag reject the Speaker's proposal four times (which has never yet happened), the procedure will be abandoned and resumed only after a new election to the Riksdag has been held (Chapter 6, Articles 4–5).

54. However, the Riksdag may of course later declare that a minister does not enjoy its confidence. Such a declaration of lack of confidence requires the concurrence of more than half the total membership of the Riksdag (Chapter 13, Article 4). Should this happen to the Prime Minister, the whole Government is discharged (Chapter 6, Articles 7–9).

The government has a collective and common responsibility for its decisions, which are agreed upon at government meetings where at least five ministers shall be present (Chapter 7, Articles 3–4).

55. As far as the election rules for the Parliament are concerned, the country is divided into some twenty-five constituencies.[22] The Riksdag comprises three hundred and ten fixed constituency seats, divided between the constituencies based on the size of population, and thirty-nine adjustment seats. The system, as described more in detail in Chapter 3, Articles 6–8 of the IG then means that parties who

22. Those are not necessarily identical at all elections, but may change due to changes in the population. The rules are to be found in the Electoral Law, Vallagen.

receive at least 4% of the votes cast throughout the whole Realm are entitled to share in the distribution of seats (as well as parties who receive fewer votes but at least 12% of the votes cast in one single constituency). The fixed constituency seats in each constituency are distributed proportionately among the parties on the basis of the election result in that constituency. The adjustment seats, then, are distributed among the parties in a way which intends to make sure (and normally in fact succeeds with this) that the distribution of all the 349 seats is proportional to the total number of votes cast throughout the whole of the Realm. Thus, compared with most other countries the election system must be described as extremely fair. Its weak point is perhaps that it does not make the creation of strong governments easy; e.g., Sweden did thus not have a majority government from May 1981 until October 2006.

§2. Political Parties, Lobbies and Interest Groups

56. As follows from what has been said above, the proportional election system makes it fairly easy for political parties to gain representation in the Parliament. At the moment, i.e., after the election in September 2014, eight parties are represented there. Those are: The conservative party (*Moderata samlingspartiet*), with 23.2% of the votes in the recent election, Christian Democrats, 4.5%, Liberal Party (*Folkpartiet*), 5.4%, Farmer's Party (*Centerpartiet*), 6.2% on the 'right', and Social Democrats, 31.2%, Green Party, 7.1% and the Leftist, former Communist Party, 5.7% on the 'left' side, together with the Nationalist Party, the "Swedish Democrats", with 12.9%.

57. A special feature of the Swedish political system, which is important to keep in mind when analysing or trying to understand it, is the dominance of the Social Democratic Party at the national level. This party has held on to the governmental power from 1932–1976 (albeit in a coalition with the Farmers 1951–1957), 1982–1991 and from 1994–2006. Together with the Green Party, it has formed a new minority government in October 2014.This situation has few equivalents in other democratic states and would normally increase the risk of corruption, which has however not so far been a big problem in Sweden.

The same parties dominate also at local and regional level, where some variations are however possible. Also at those levels, the same electoral rules apply, though in a slightly modified form; exact details on this are to be found in the lengthy Electoral Law (*Vallagen*, 1997:157), in particular Chapter 18.

58. The existing law today concerning financial support for political parties is the law on state support or aid of political parties (*lagen om statligt stöd till politiska partier*, 1972:625). Apart from that, there is also since 1996 a law on the registration of the economic interests and commitments of the Members of Parliament from 1996 (1996:810), which is however not compulsory but entirely based on voluntary participation of the MP's. According to the law, though, the MP's following the instructions have to reveal their incomes and activities. The idea behind the voluntary participation appears to be that the voters would have less confidence in

MP's not participating, but so far no study has been made on whether this is actually the case.

59. However, a governmental committee in 2004 proposed a new law in order to make the whole area more regulated and transparent. The document or report containing this proposal, a new law on the publication of the incomes of political parties and electoral candidates (proposed to enter into force on 1 January 2006), *Allmänhetens insyn i partiers och valkandidaters intäkter* (The public openness of the incomes of parties and electoral candidates), Statens offentliga utredningar (SOU)[23] 2004:22, is thus in many ways the logical point of departure for discussing those questions. The existing law as well as the proposed ones are of course national ones, but their rules cover candidates to the national parliament as well as local and regional assemblies and also the European Parliament.

60. No limits on contributions to political parties exist at the moment. The proposal of 2004 never entered into force, but meant that each party should make an annual public account of its incomes and that, at the same time, each candidate who had been elected to any of the assemblies mentioned above (i.e., national parliament, local or regional assembly or the European Parliament), should be obliged to make a public declaration on how the campaign was financed. This last proposal should be viewed in the light of the increased scope for personal campaigning that has been introduced since 1998, due to changes in the Electoral Law.

61. At the moment, no limitations exist for how much may a natural person contribute to a single party or candidate. The new proposal is that the value of each contribution and the name of the donor shall be made public if the total contribution during the respective relevant period adds up to a total of SEK 20,000 or more. Apart from that, the total sum of all anonymous contributions shall also be made public. Since those rules have not entered into force, however, Sweden has been criticized by the Council of Europe.

62. Awaiting this proposed legislation, an agreement between all the main political parties from 1980, confirmed in 2000, means that the parties are obliged to reveal their sources of income at the national level, whenever asked to do so by the media or representatives of the public. Information concerning the economic interests of any member of the government is public since 1995.

63. As a reaction to the criticism mentioned above, the government in 2013 proposed new rules that limited the possibilities for parties to accept economical contributions but still allowed anonymous donations, which was highly controversial.[24] Furthermore, contrary to the recommendations from the Council of Europe, no presentation of the money received was required until 2015, i.e., after the general election in September 2014. The proposal was altered after certain discussion and the

23. Statens Offentliga Utredningar, i.e., Official Government Reports.
24. Ds 2013:31, Allmänhetens insyn i partiers och valkandidaters finansiering.

rules, decided by the Parliament in March 2014, now state that parties who will continue to receive anonymous contributions will not enjoy state support.[25]

64. No rules exist concerning which persons, organizations, classes of person, or classes of organization, if any, are expressly forbidden from contributing. The general rules against bribery and corruption in the Penal Code would apply if such crimes would be suspected. Those rules have been changed and sharpened in recent years, as a result of new rules and conventions within the EU and the Council of Europe.

65. The state aid to political parties, which is annually in total circa SEK 250 million, goes to the parties represented in the Parliament or at local or regional level in a relation which is proportional to their size, i.e., their results in the last election. For most of them, this is today their main source of income.

66. Some party foundations or think tanks exist, supporting notably the conservative party. What is however a bigger and more important issue, not least given the long reign of the Social Democratic Party, is the long and strong political and economical bond between that party and the national trade union organization (*Landsorganizationen, LO*).

67. How much money to allocate to individual candidates, or parties, or other organizations is determined on the basis of percentage of popular vote and number of seats in the parliament at the same time, since the election system is strictly proportional.

68. Public funds are given as a support for each mandate in the parliament, with a total in 2004 of SEK 282,450 for each mandate in the Parliament yearly. Each party with 4% of the votes is thus given SEK 4,928,200 as a base, and then SEK 20,650 for each mandate, as far as the national support is concerned. (This adds up to circa SEK 150 million each year.) For the local and regional bodies, the rules are more complicated. This state aid to the political parties has existed since 1965.

69. No restrictions concerning political campaign activities of civil servants and other public employees exist as such, which is worth noting. This is typically considered as part of the freedom of speech, though it goes without saying that the public confidence for leading civil servants or judges would not survive a strong political bias from any of them.

70. No real restrictions seem to exist concerning 'official' use of public resources by elected officials during election campaign periods or at other times (e.g., use of broadcast and print media, use of public buildings, use of official motor vehicles, aircraft and other transportation), but it may be noted that the use made of the Prime

25. KU 2013/14:35, Ökad insyn i partiers och valkandidaters finansiering. All parties except the right-wing Sweden Democrats agreed to the new rules.

Minister of the official government airplane in the preparations for the election campaign 2002 for internal party affairs was contested. Thus, excessive use of such resources could probably be considered as a misuse of public funds.[26]

71. Measures do exist to protect challenger candidates from the media and communication advantages believed in some countries to favour incumbents, but mainly in the form of the obligation of the state radio and TV (public service, not allowing advertising) to observe strict neutrality during electoral campaigns. Since commercial broadcasting is becoming ever more important, the relevance of this legislation may be questioned.

72. There used to be restrictions on the use of broadcast media in political campaigns in the form of a voluntary agreement between almost all media companies and networks not to allow pure political advertising (which does however apply permanently). It is only the state radio and TV, as well as TV 4 (a private TV company with a national concession) that is regulated by law in this respect. However, in the election campaign of 2010, advertising for the political parties in all media was allowed for the first time.

73. Registration requirements exist for political parties, as well as for candidates and other organizations. For the first two categories, this is rather strictly regulated in the electoral law, Chapter 5, according to which all parties and candidates must be supported by a number of persons and applications for new parties made a certain time before the elections.

74. No restrictions or registration requirements exist for domestic or foreign lobbyists, since the exercise of that activity is covered by the right to free exercise of trade or profession. Concerning other restrictions on campaign activities of lobbyists, only general criminal rules regulate this area.

75. Gifts to government officials are not expressly forbidden, but the rules are quite strict, partly because the limit of what constitutes a bribe in terms of a gift to a public official (or a business associate) is very low, as a consequence of rules in the penal code, statements in their preparatory works and settled case law from the courts. Apart from that, administrative rules exist according to which all gifts to ministers are registered in a public register and data base. The new proposals means that the parties shall be legally responsible for the reporting described above. Awaiting that, the public prosecutors are responsible for sanctioning violations of the rules.

26. A similar discussion arose when the Minister of Finance Mr Ringholm in 2004 used the government's plane in order to fly back from a match at the European Championship in Football in Portugal to a Trade Union Conference. The question whether national legislation does provide for enforcement action/penalties against corrupt practices committed abroad (*outside* national jurisdiction) is a general issue related to penal law. For a closer study, see Criminal act, criminal jurisdiction and Criminal Justice, a doctoral dissertation by Christoffer Wong, Faculty of Law, University of Lund 2004 (published by Polpress, Krakow, *Poland*). It may be mentioned that there is a special rule in this respect in Ch. 19, Art. 13 of the Penal Code (*Brottsbalken*).

76. The only example of a prominent case of enforcement that comes to mind concerns a conservative member of Parliament, who in 1996 had to leave the Parliament because he had been on the pay roll of a big local wood producing company while being member of Parliament, without the nature of the work he did for the company being clarified. In 2005, the President of the Social democratic Youth Organization was asked to clarify if he used funds designed for other activities, a total of SEK 76,000, for his election campaign to the European Parliament in 2004. It may be noted that members of parliament are allowed to have other jobs, for instance as lawyers. In recent years, some prominent lawyers in Stockholm have been members of the Parliament for the Social democrats or Christian Democrats while continuing their practice; a notable example is Mr Peter Althin, MP for the Christian Democrats, defending among others Mijailo Mijailovic, convicted assassin of former Foreign Minister Anna Lindh.

77. This low degree of corruption may be surprising given the lack of transparency and regulation in this field (which may be surprising in itself given the traditional Swedish attachment to transparency). However, transparency in other areas of public life, e.g., in relation to individual incomes in general, has so far been considered sufficient here. It remains to be seen if it will be sufficient also in the future.

§3. Referendum as an Alternative to Representative Democracy

78. According to Chapter 8, Article 4 IG, provisions concerning the holding of a consultative referendum throughout the whole of the Realm and the procedure for holding a referendum on a matter of fundamental law are laid down in law. This means that when a majority in Parliament is in favour of organizing a referendum on a certain issue, this will be organized through a special law, which relates only to this specific event.[27] Thus, as follows also indirectly from Chapter 8, Article 16, referendas are obviously allowed in Swedish law, but it is also clear from the abovementioned rules in Chapter 3 IG that representative democracy, exercised on the basis of proportional elections, is the main rule under which Swedish democracy is exercised. It would perhaps have been better if this had been clearly addressed somewhere in the Constitutional text, since the demands for an increased use of referendas have been frequent in recent years. Since the 1920s, five national referendas have been organized, but only the one concerning membership in the EU in November 1994 may have been said to be quite fair from the point of view that it was both a clear option between yes and no, that the number of voters or the electoral turnout in other words was high and that there were no other legally doubtful issues that caused difficulties or doubts on the result.[28] Also the result was reasonably clear (52.4% yes *v.* 46.7% no-votes).

27. Whether this is really compatible with the prohibition against legislation in individual cases that follows from Ch. 11, Art. 8 IG is actually quite doubtful, but the issue has never been legally contested.
28. The other five national referendas that have been organized have concerned the allowance of sales of alcoholic beverages in 1922, whether to drive on the right or left side of the road in 1955, the organization of the pension system in 1957, whether to continue using nuclear energy in 1980 and membership in the EMU in 2003. There are a number of problems related to all those. In 1922, a

79. Local referendas, on the other hand, are becoming more and more frequent, in particular in connection with local elections, as shown most recently in Gothenburg in 2014. This is logical given not least the development and high degree of use of internet-related technology in Sweden. From a Constitutional and democratic point of view, that development as such seems highly promising and positive, whereas national referendas have so far tended to be much more problematic.[29]

very narrow majority voted against prohibition, In 1955, 89% of the voters wished to continue driving on the left side of the road, which did not stop the political majority from changing to right-road driving in 1967, Both in 1957 and 1980, the choice between three different options blurred the campaigns and the referendas in fact created more new problems than it solved old ones. Concerning the EMU referendum, it was held mainly for domestic political reasons, with a weak legal base (see Nergelius, in Luif (2007), and it was also particularly ill-fated due to the assassination of Foreign Minister Anna Lindh. Originally, there was no majority in the Parliament for organizing that referendum, but that situation changed in 1997 through a surprise move by former opposition leader and PM, current foreign minister Carl Bildt, as explained below in Ch. 3, § 4.

29. In the spring of 2010, a new situation occurred, when the left-wing opposition agreed to, should it form a government after the election in September 2010, let the parliament decide to let twenty-six municipalities around Stockholm decide in a joint referendum whether to build a new motorway around Stockholm, whether those municipalities like it or not. This was mainly a way to solve their internal disagreement and the arrangement looks constitutionally very doubtful.

Chapter 2. Head of State

80. Sweden has been a monarchy for a very long time, since before 1523. Still, it may of course be questioned whether this hereditary regime, with all its privileges, is really adapted to a modern, secular and highly egalitarian society such as today's Sweden. But since regular opinion polls show the support for the monarchy as an institution to be continuously strong among the citizens (with some 70% regular in favour of it) that seems to be the case and arguments in favour of republic are not really seen as realistic.[30] Still, it may be noted that the popularity of the Monarchy did not rise in June 2010, a week before the planned wedding between Crown Princess Victoria and Mr Daniel Westling. Neither has the subsequent arrival of new princesses had any significant impact in this respect.

81. The rules regulating the monarchy are to be found in Chapter 5 IG and in the Act of Succession. Those rules and in particular the ones from 1974 may be seen as aiming at giving the monarch as little power as possible, in contrast to the old Constitution from 1809, but at the same time preserving the representative nature, character and tasks of the institution. This solution goes back to a well-known compromise between the Social Democrats and the right-wing parties from 1971 (*Torekovskompromissen*), according to which the monarchy should be preserved but totally stripped of its former, formal powers.

82. It follows from Chapter 1, Article 5 IG that the King or Queen who occupies the throne of Sweden in accordance with the Act of Succession (i.e., who is a legitimate heir or possessor of the throne) shall be the Head of State. Which functions do then remain for the Monarch, the king or Head of State[31] to exercise, once this compromise had been reached in 1971?

83. According to Chapter 6, Article 6, (s)he presides at a special Council of State meeting when the Government changes hands. In a similar manner, he or she[32] is the one who opens the annual Parliament session, normally in the beginning of October (The Riksdag Act Chapter 1, Article 4). Slightly surprising, perhaps, he is also president of The Advisory Council on Foreign Affairs (*Utrikesnämnden*), an important body for discussions on foreign policy between the government and the opposition.

84. According to Chapter 5, Article 1 IG, the Head of State shall be kept informed by the PM concerning the affairs of the Realm, when so required through a special Council of State under the chairmanship of the Head of State (which does

---

30. In fact, today the majority of MP's seems to be in favour of a republic, at least in their statements, but no party is actively pursuing this issue.
31. It follows from Ch. 5 IG that the King (Monarch) and the Head of State are not necessarily the same person, but since that has been the case so far, there seems to be no reason to expect any other regulation in the future.
32. The Crown Princess Victoria is likely to succeed her father when his mandate ends, i.e., when he resigns or dies (he was 60 years old in 2006). The Act of Succession was changed in 1979 in this respect, enabling a female Monarch.

however happen very rarely, if ever). It is difficult to imagine that a very busy Prime Minister would regularly find the time to inform the Head of State on various items, but if the Monarch does not get informed about important events in due time, that may give rise to criticism against the government, which was the case after the terrible *Tsunami* disaster in December 2004. Having this in mind, also the chairmanship of the Head of State in the Advisory Council on Foreign Affairs may be justified with the need for the King to be informed about conditions in foreign parts of the world before his trips and in similar situations, though this could perhaps have been settled in some other way. Still, this line of reasoning illustrates the representative task of the Head of State, who represents Sweden externally, but who should as far as possible refrain from having any position of his own in controversial issues.

85. A remnant of the old kind of privileges, that always used to be given to the Monarchy, may be found in Chapter 5, Article 7 IG, according to which the King can never be prosecuted for his actions. This immunity from penal law does not include other members of the royal family and it does not extend to civil law, under which the King, his family and the royal court may be sued under various actions.

86. The formal requirements for anyone to act as Head of State are regulated in Chapter 5, Articles 2–6 IG. It follows from those rules that in order to serve in that function, a person must be a Swedish citizen who has reached the age of 18.[33] If, by reason of ill health, foreign travel or for any other cause, the King is prevented from performing his duties, that Member of the Royal House under the valid order of succession who is not prevented there from shall assume and perform the duties of Head of State in the capacity of Regent *ad interim*, Chapter 5, Article 3. Should for some reason the Royal House become extinct, or the King die or abdicate before the heir to the throne has attained the age of 18, the Parliament will under Chapter 5, Article 4 IG appoint a Regent to perform the duties of Head of State (as well as a Deputy Regent) until further notice. And if the King has been continuously prevented for six months from performing his duties, or has failed to perform them, the Government shall notice the Parliament, who then determines whether the King shall be deemed to have abdicated. According to the Constitution of 1809, the Parliament in such a situation as the ones mentioned here had to appoint a new Royal House, but in today's situation it seems clear that the Parliament could choose between that option and, on the other hand, to change by introducing a Republic instead.

87. This leads us over to the Act of Succession, the most old-fashioned of the four Constitutional acts, in its language as well as in its contents. According to IG Chapter 1, Article 5, section 2, the provisions of IG that relate to the King shall apply to the Queen should a Queen be head of state. This reform, aiming primarily at equality between men and women in society in a more general sense, was introduced in 1979, since the oldest child of the King Carl XVI Gustav turned out to be

33. This is the reason why a big ceremony was held in the Royal *Castle* of Stockholm on the 14 Jul. 1995, when Crown Princess Victoria had her 18th birthday.

a girl (Crown Princess Victoria). At the same time, changes were then also introduced into the Act of Succession. Under its first Article, the right of succession to the throne of Sweden is vested in the male and female descendants of King Carl XVI Gustaf, with a precedence for older siblings and their descendants over younger siblings and their respective descendants. And under Article 2, all provisions of the Act of Succession relating to the King shall relate to the Queen should she be Head Of State.

88. The rather old-fashioned nature of some of the provisions that still relate to the Monarchy may be illustrated by its Article 5, according to which a prince or princess of the Swedish Royal House may not marry unless the Government has given its consent thereto upon an application from the King; should the prince or princess marry without such consent, he or she forfeits the right of succession for himself, his children and their descendants. In the same way, no prince or princess may according to Article 8 become the sovereign ruler of a foreign state whether by election, succession or marriage without the consent of the King and the Riksdag; should that occur, neither the prince/princess or their descendants shall be entitled to succeed to the throne of Sweden. And according to Article 7, the heir to the throne may not even undertake any travel abroad without the knowledge and consent of the King.

89. Still, the most old-fashioned rule of the whole Swedish Constitution, without any doubt, is Article 4, according to which the following applies in relation to the religious activities of the Royal family:

> In accordance with the express provision of Article 2 of the Instrument of Government of 1809 that the King shall always profess the pure evangelical faith, as adopted and explained in the unaltered Confession of Augsburg and in the Resolution of the Uppsala meeting of the year 1593, princes and princesses of the Royal House shall be brought up in that same faith and within the Realm. Any member of the Royal Family not professing this faith shall be excluded from all rights of succession.

90. This means, when a more normal and contemporary language is used, that all members of the royal family who want to keep their right to inherit the throne must profess the pure evangelical (i.e., protestant) faith. This means for instance that it is doubtful whether the young princess Leonore, born in February 2014 and daughter of princess Madeleine, will ever be able to inherit the throne, given that her father is a catholic. Thus, no freedom of religion exists for the royal family.[34] Apart from that regrettable fact, the still valid provision expresses values and attitudes which are simply not in line with contemporary attitudes of the Swedish society. For that reason, it is surprising that the Committee preparing a Constitutional

34. It may of course be questioned whether members of the royal family enjoys other human rights like the freedom of speech or the right to vote. A correct statement seems to be that the royals are not deprived of such rights, but do not use them due to tradition; see e.g., Warnling-Nerep/Lagerqvist Veloz Roca/Reichel, Statsrättens grunder, p. 94.

reform for 2010 has not been given the task to look into those or any other rules relating to the Monarchy; it ought to be possible for such a committee to discuss changes in some apparently obsolete rules without questioning the Monarchy as such, as an institution (which the main political parties have agreed not to do).

Chapter 3. The Legislature

§1. The Organ of State

91. Ever since the unicameral Parliament was introduced in 1970, elections to three levels of political decision-making, i.e., Parliament, municipalities and county councils, have been held simultaneously, which means that they are held on the third Sunday of September, originally every third year but since 1994 every fourth year. This manner of organizing the elections is far from the only one possible, but a number of committees – the latest one in 2002[35] – has argued against introducing separate election days for local and national elections, mainly because it might lead to a lower electoral turnout in the local elections.[36] However, in 2010, two changes did suddenly appear, in the shape of a possibility for the municipalities to organize separate elections between the regular elections every fourth year – which will however not liberate them from the obligation to organize new, regular ones 'next time around', so to speak – and, as mentioned above, that the elections will be moved to the second Sunday in September starting from 2014.

92. If we should here focus on the national elections, we may note the Parliament is, according to Chapter 3, Article 1 IG appointed by means of free, secret and direct elections. Voting in such elections is by party, with an option for the voter to express a preference for a particular candidate. The fact that those elections are 'free' does of course mean that each voter gives his vote freely to the party that he or she finds best, having – hopefully – studied their respective programs carefully. The secrecy refers to the fact that the voter does not have to reveal how he votes, which corresponds to the right guaranteed by Chapter 2, Article 2 IG of not having to reveal ones political opinion. At election time, the voter may pick as many party lists as he wishes, but in the electoral booth, he may only put one into each envelope (one for each election). Should he or she wish to openly declare his preference for a certain party, that is of course also allowed.

93. The directness involved is perhaps the most important or peculiar criterion, since it relates to the proportional electoral system. (It does in other words not relate to a widespread use of referendas, as explained above.)

94. According to Chapter 3, Article 4 IG, every Swedish citizen who is currently or who has ever been domiciled within the Realm is entitled to vote in the Parliamentary election, given that he or she has attained the age of 18 on or before the election day. The rule seems old-fashioned from the point of view that it is today quite easy to imagine a Swedish citizen who has never been domiciled within the

35. See the official report SOU 2002:42, Den gemensamma valdagen och andra valfrågor.
36. There is undoubtedly a political reality behind this commitment to a procedure decided in the 1970s, namely that the Social Democrats fear losing influence in many municipalities if the elections to those would take place independently of the national elections, during which the Social Democratic Party, an unusually effective political power-machine, may use its whole 'artillery' and resources also to influence the outcome of the local elections.

Realm, in which case it is hard to justify why that person should not be entitled to vote. Difficult cases are to be decided on the basis of an electoral roll drawn up before the election; the more detailed rules concerning that roll are to be found in the Electoral Law (*Vallagen*).[37] The same criteria apply in order to be elected as an MP, according to Chapter 3, Article 4, section 3.

95. Thus, a one-chamber system, which is closely related to the proportional electoral system, has existed since 1970. The historical background to this is that the right-wing parties were in favour of such a reform ever since 1945. Having faced a drawback in the local elections 1966, when the issue did suddenly become important, the Social Democrats accepted to change its position on the issue, though the proportional system and the simultaneous election day as well as the role of the Monarchy were then also parts of the 'package' or reform. The sudden need for this reform may today seem slightly surprising, since the period of the bicameral legislature, 1866–1970, was historically extremely successful for Sweden. But sometimes political changes are not entirely logical in the way they happen.

96. Anyway, as mentioned above the electoral system is based on the division of the Realm into specific constituencies for the parliamentary elections. According to Chapter 3, Article 6, the Riksdag comprises three hundred and ten fixed constituency seats and thirty-nine adjustment seats. While the fixed constituency seats are distributed among the constituencies on the basis of a calculation of the relationship between the number of persons entitled to vote in each constituency and the total number of persons entitled to vote throughout the whole of the Realm, which will always be beneficial for the main, biggest parties, the function and idea of the thirty-nine adjustment seats may be said to be to compensate the smaller parties for their 'losses' there, in relation to their total numbers of votes throughout the whole country (see Chapter 3, Article 8 for more details). As follows from Chapter 3, Article 7, only parties who have received at least 4% of the votes cast throughout the whole country is entitled to take a share in the distribution of seats. Since the system is proportional, a party that has for instance won 5% of the votes shall also get 5% of the seats. One exception may lead to deviations – though it has so far never happened – namely if a party should win at least 12% of the votes in one particular constituency, but less than 4% in the country as a whole. Apart from that possibility, however, the system is 'working' from the point of view that it really leads to the effects wished for in terms of proportionality and, thus, a fair result. On the other hand, it is clear that it does not facilitate the birth of strong governments, possessing a strong majority in the Parliament. When a majority government entered in October 2006, supported by 178 MP's, this was actually the first time since May 1981 that such a government ruled!

97. According to Chapter 3, Article 1, the voting in the elections is by party, with an option for the voter to express a preference for a particular candidate. So far, however, that latter possibility, which was introduced in 1998, has not had any big importance. It is possible that it would grow more important should the possibility

37. See in particular Ch. 7, Art. 1 of that law.

for extraordinary elections be wider. So far, extraordinary elections have surprisingly enough never taken place in Sweden, which may be due to the fact that if they should occur, the ordinary election will take place as planned anyway (see Chapter 3, Articles 3–4 in combination).[38] In the directives to the committee preparing a Constitutional reform, a change of this rule was envisaged, which could perhaps mean that should an extraordinary election take place, the new ordinary election should not take place within four years from the date of that election. It seems likely that such a move would have been able to vitalize the political climate of the country and the party system, in particular since it would in reality make a distinction or division between national and local elections more likely, but no change has so far occurred.

§2. Legal Status

98. It follows from what has been said above that the Parliament or Riksdag is a unicameral body which is elected in ordinary elections in September every fourth year, with a possibility for extraordinary elections that has so far never been used.

99. According to Chapter 4, Article 1 IG, the Riksdag convenes in session every year. Sessions are held in Stockholm, unless otherwise determined by the Riksdag or the Speaker. As follows from Chapter 1, Article 2 of the Riksdag Act, every parliamentary or Riksdag session continues until the start of the next session, though the starting date of such a session will depend on whether an election has taken place or not. Should that be the case, the Parliament as mentioned above will convene on the fifteenth day after election day while otherwise, in years when no ordinary election is held, a new session starts on a day in September determined by the Parliament in advance (i.e., before its summer recess).[39]

100. Regardless of when the Parliament meets for the first time, whether it is after an election or otherwise, a roll-call of members is taken at the first meeting of the chamber (Chapter 1, Article 3 of the Riksdag Act). When elections have been held, the Speaker as well as the First, Second and Third Deputy Speakers are elected

38. Concerning the rules for extraordinary elections in general, it may be noted that they may only be called when three months have passed since the newly elected Parliament was convened after the former election. The Government is also barred from calling an extraordinary election when its ministers remain at their posts, after they have been formally discharged, pending assumption of office by a new government. See Ch. 3, Art. 4, s. 2 for further details.

39. This means that formally speaking, the Parliamentary session (*riksmöte*) is always convened, though it would of course be impossible to ask of the MP's that they should be in session in Stockholm for fifty-two weeks of the year. Instead, the Riksdag Act prescribes (Ch. 2, Art. 6) that the Speaker will determine what breaks of a week or more that shall be made in the work of the Chamber during the current session; normally, the session is for instance interrupted for summer and Christmas breaks and during certain other weeks. He may also decide, upon a request by 115 MP's or by the Government, to interrupt a parliamentary recess, in which case a meeting of the Chamber shall be held within ten days from the submission of such a request.

at that same meeting, for the whole electoral period.[40] The formal opening of a Parliamentary session, then, according to Chapter 1, Article 4 takes place at a special meeting of the Chamber held no later than the third day of the session. At that meeting, the Head of State formally declares the session open at the invitation of the Speaker and the PM will deliver a Government policy statement.

101. According to Chapter 2, Article 4 of the Riksdag Act, the meetings of the Chamber are open to the public, though the Parliament may decide that a meeting shall be held behind closed doors for reasons of national security or relations with other states (which has however not happened since the Second World War). Concerning the debates, it may be noted that the Chamber will convene in response to a summons from the Speaker, which shall be posted fourteen hours in advance (Chapter 2, Article 5). According to Chapter 2, Article 7, the Speaker shall prepare an order paper for each meeting listing all matters on the table of the Chamber. During the meetings, every MP as well as every minister is entitled to speak freely on all matters under deliberation, Chapter 2, Article 10, though limits may be prescribed to the number of interventions that a speaker may make during the deliberation of a matter and the duration of such interventions (Chapter 2, Article 14). In Chapter 2, Article 12 of the Riksdag Act also other possible restrictions are mentioned; thus, no one may express himself at a meeting improperly concerning another person or indulge in personal insult or otherwise conduct himself by word or deed in a manner not consistent with good order. Should that happen, the Speaker may prohibit that particular MP from speaking for the remainder of the debate.[41]

102. Generally speaking, the parliamentary debates in Sweden are rather lame, without the intensity that is to be found for example in UK. A reform of the rules, enabling for instance more spontaneous, unprepared comments or speeches to be made, is now considered within the Parliament. That would probably be a step in the right direction in this respect.

103. Concerning the legal status of the MP's, it has already been noted that they are elected for four years (IG Chapter 3, Article 3). It should also be noted that an MP (or an alternate[42]) under Chapter 4, Article 10 may exercise his mandate

40. See Ch. 8, Art. 1 of the Riksdag Act. Should only one person be nominated, the election procedure is uncomplicated, but in other case individual votes from all MP's are given. Should no one has obtained a majority after two votes, a third and final round will be held between the two candidates with the most votes in the second round. In that, third and final round, the candidate with the highest number of votes will be elected. At least once, in 1979, there has actually been a contest between the representative or candidate of the narrow, right-wing majority and the Social Democrat suggested by that party, Mr Bengtsson (who was in the end elected and then remained in office until 1988).

41. In September 2014, almost all the articles in the Riksdag Act changed their numbers, though very little if any of the substance of the Act was changed. The reasons, if any, for this unnecessary change, that will not be dealt with here, remain highly unclear.

42. The conditions for installing alternates are regulated in Ch. 4, Art. 9 IG, according to which such a person may be nominated whenever an MP is acting as Speaker or minister, or simply when the MP is on leave of absence.

notwithstanding any official duty or other similar obligation incumbent upon him.[43] The formal conditions for being an MP are identical with the ones that qualify voters in the national elections, i.e., that they are 18 years old and have once been domiciled within the Realm (see IG, Chapter 3, Article 4 and 10, see also Chapter 4, Article 11).

104. An MP may not resign his mandate without the Parliament's consent, as follows from Chapter 4, Article 11. However, according to section 3 of that Article, he may be deprived of his mandate if he has proved himself manifestly unfit to hold such a mandate by reason of a criminal act, a decision which needs to be made by a court.[44]

105. Should an MP be suspected for a crime, an immunity rule of slightly limited value is to be found in IG Chapter 4, Article 12, according to which no person may take legal action against a person who holds or has held a mandate as an MP, deprive him of his liberty or restrict his movements within the realm on account of any act or statement made in the exercise of his mandate, unless the Parliament gives its consent to such an action through a formal decision with five sixths majority of the concurring MP's. This is however only applicable when the MP stays, physically, in one of the bodies of the Parliament. In other cases when an MP is suspected of having committed a crime, rules concerning arrest, detention or remand are applied only if he admits guilt or has been caught in the act, or if the minimum penalty for the offence is imprisonment for a minimum of two years (which is only the case for very severe crimes). It may be noted that other kinds of deprivations of liberty, e.g., for medical reasons, are not included. This may seem slightly strange, given that the purpose of the rule is to protect the integrity and independence of the Parliament as an institution.

§3. COMPETENCES

106. The two most important competences of the Swedish Parliament are undoubtedly its legislative (Chapter 8 IG) as well as its budgetary (Chapter 9) powers, which will now be dealt with.

I. Legislation: Further on Chapter 8 of the Instrument of Government

107. As has already been mentioned, laws are normally passed or decided by a decision supported by the majority of voting MP's (IG Chapter 4, Article 7). A few

43. A similar provision ought to exist for MEP's, but that has not yet been introduced (which could be seen as an example of Sweden's weak European commitment but could of course also be totally coincidental.
44. This actually happened to a conservative MP in 1997, after he had been sentenced for an economic crime.

words on the hierarchy of norms, with the four Constitutional Acts at the top, followed by the Riksdag Act and rules on religious communities, then by ordinary laws, regulations and decrees have been mentioned in Part I above, which also dealt with the complicated rules concerning delegation of legislative powers. Another few more words shall now be said.

108. The main reason why Chapter 8 of the Constitution is so difficult and complicated is perhaps its ambition to include and cover all those different kinds of rules. Furthermore, delegation from the Parliament to the Government, sometimes followed by further so-called *sub-delegation* to various public authorities, is the main technique used for achieving those purposes, as opposed to many other countries, where the Constitution more aims at regulating the line between the different competences of the Government and the Parliament, which may be explained by a wish for flexibility in combination with a historical respect and reverence, on this particular point, for the Constitution of 1809.[45] Still, the result of this, politically uncontested regulation is a severe lack of clarity, which almost all public Swedish lawyers do today condemn or criticize.

109. Indirectly, a point of departure concerning legislation is to be found in Chapter 11, Article 4 IG, which states that no judicial or administrative function may be performed by the Parliament except to the extent that this follows from the Constitutional acts or the Riksdag Act. This means, in other words, that laws must be general to their nature or, as it may also be formulated, that a law must be possible, at least theoretically, to apply in more than one case, although it may in reality be enacted with one specific case in view. Some laws have in fact been set aside by courts or not approved by the Law Council because they have not met that requirement, which does however not mean that laws require that all individuals must be treated alike.[46] Nevertheless, this requirement limits the freedom of action of the Parliament quite drastically.[47]

110. As mentioned above in Part I, the form of law is compulsory for various legal acts, notably in the fields of private or civil law (Chapter 8, Article 2, section 1), taxes and burdensome public law in general, including of course penal law (Article 2, section 2), provisions on organization of a national referendum (Article 2, section 5, the compatibility of which with Chapter 11, Article 8 could actually be questioned, though the provision does not address individual legal subjects), principles governing the organization and working procedures of the local authorities and local taxation, as well as relating to the competence of local authorities and their responsibilities and the division of the Realm into local government districts (Article 2, section 3) not to be forgotten. The same is true for procedural law (Chapter 11, Articles 2 and 5, see also Chapter 11, Article 1 for some further details).

45. Cfr Nergelius, *supra*, p. 75 ss with further references.
46. See *further* Nergelius, *ibid.* p. 78 ss with details and examples.
47. Other countries may have different traditions in this respect. For instance, in Denmark legislation concerning specific cases may be passed by the Parliament (*Folketinget*). The importance of the Swedish regulation, though far from unique, should thus be pointed out.

Those provisions are as such clear and uncomplicated; once again, the difficulties in Chapter 8 are related to the division of competencies between and the (system for) delegation of legislative power from the Parliament to the Government, as stated above in Part II.

II. Budgetary and Financial Power: Instrument of Government Chapter 9

111. The headline of Chapter 9 IG is Financial power (*Finansmakten*), which could be said to mean simply the right for the state to decide on its incomes and expenses, tasks that are normally divided into taxation and budgetary regulation. Though in a way two sides of the same coin, those two activities are from a strictly constitutional point of view different which, in relation to what was said in the previous Chapter, is perhaps best illustrated by the fact that while decisions on taxes do always need to be made through a law, that is not the case concerning budgetary decisions.[48] Within this rather short Chapter, however, also several other issues are regulated, of which we may note the position and competencies of the National Bank (*Riksbanken*), that was changed most recently in 1998. Also another huge, partly constitutional reform concerning the budgetary process, which has to a certain extent affected this Chapter and therefore needs to be studied here, was launched in the mid-1990s.

112. The competence of the Parliament to decide upon state taxes is mentioned already in Chapter 1, Article 4 IG. This competence has old historical roots; there was a famous statement in the Constitution of 1809 which talked about 'the ancient right of the Swedish people to be taxed' and in a way that spirit is still present in Swedish thinking about taxation issues. It is also a well-known fact that taxes at least for individuals are still very high in Sweden. At the same time, it must be noted that municipal taxes are for almost all working persons in Sweden a much higher expense than the state tax, since everyone pays municipal taxes while state tax is reserved for people with high incomes and companies. Municipal taxes are also more important from the point of view that the main part of the well-known Swedish welfare – schools, hospitals, elderly living and other things – is actually organized at a municipal and not at a national level. Nevertheless, the issue of municipal tax, which will be further discussed below in Part III, is hardly mentioned at all in the Constitution.

48. Those are also from certain other points of view surprisingly informal and unregulated. Thus, there is no rule in the Constitution or elsewhere concerning the formal conditions under which the Government is to hand over the budget to the Parliament and no legal requirement anywhere concerning the balance in the budget between incomes and expenses. It should be noted that according to Ch. 9, Art. 11 IG, further rules concerning the competence and responsibilities of the Riksdag and Government in respect of the adoption of the national budget may be laid down in the Riksdag Act and separate, ordinary legislation. This has in particular been the case with a law on the state budget from 1996 (1996:1059).

113. Also the issue of taxation as such is scarcely mentioned within Chapter 9, which focuses instead on the budgetary process and the competences of the Parliament and the Government within that process. In somewhat broader terms, that relation could be said to mean that the assets of the state so to speak 'do belong' to the Parliament, who decides on how to make use of them, while the Government is more like an executive body, that may implement and execute decisions of the Government within this area. This relationship is particularly clearly expressed in Chapter 9, Article 8 IG, which states that funds and other assets of the State are at the disposal of the Government (apart from assets intended for the Parliament or its specific authorities). Also Chapter 9, Articles 1 and 3 makes clear that state funds may not be used otherwise than as determined by the Parliament.[49]

114. Concerning the budgetary procedure, it follows from Chapter 9, Article 2 that the Government submits proposals for a national budget to the Parliament, that according to Article 3 and 7 approves the use of state funds for different purposes by adopting a budget in accordance with the rules laid down in Chapter 9, Articles 3–5. According to those rules, the Parliament adopts a national budget for the next budget year,[50] with an estimate of public revenue and an appropriation for specific purposes (though certain appropriations may be made for other periods than the budgetary ones, Chapter 9, Article 3, section 2).

115. Those rules are basically the same that were introduced in 1974, but as far as the details and modalities of the process are concerned a major reform was initiated, as stated above, in 1996. While the budgetary proposal from the Government was before given on the 10 January, it is now handed over no later than 20 September (or as soon as possible after the election, should it be election year).[51] This above all gives the Parliament a possibility to focus on budgetary issues during the fall and on legislation during its spring session, which is generally considered to be more efficient.

116. Within the process and within the work of the Parliament, the position of the Finance Committee (*Finansutskottet*) has been much strengthened. According to Chapter 3, Article 7 of the Riksdag Act, it may now, in all issues concerning economic policy, introduce proposals in the Parliament also on matters falling within the competence of other committees. And under Chapter 4, Article 8 of that same Act, it shall be given the opportunity to comment on proposals from any other parliamentary committee whenever the proposal may have significant future repercussions for public revenue and expenditure.[52]

49. Within the Constitutional doctrine, it is however generally accepted that the Government may refuse to execute an envisaged payment and thus go against the Parliament on certain details; see Nergelius, *supra*, p. 103 with details and references.
50. Which is now, since 1996, the same as the Calendar Year; see the Riksdag Act Ch. 3, Art. 2, s. 1.
51. In 2006, the new Government, which had been presented and started its work on the 6 October, presented the budget already the 16 October. It goes without saying that in such a situation, the possibility of the Government to deviate from the policy of the old Government is very limited indeed.
52. The general rule on the tasks and competences of that committee is to be found in Ch. 4, Art. 6, supplementary provision 2 of the Riksdag Act.

117. The reform also means that a kind of framework decisional model has been introduced, according to which the Parliament, when it has received the budgetary proposal, shall make a decision concerning allocation and spending limits for twenty-seven different sectors or 'frames' of expenditure into which the budget is divided. At the same time, the Parliament will also decide on tax changes for the next year. This means that also the future incomes may be summed up, which will give the Parliament a much better overview of the future economic situation than before.

118. When the parliamentary committees have dealt with the various proposals, sector by sector so to speak,[53] the regulation in Chapter 5, Article 12, section 4 of the Riksdag Act means that decisions concerning appropriations for the current budget year which affect expenditure limits may not be made before a decision has been made by the Parliament approving adjustments of the expenditure limits. First, then, each committee proposes in a report which expenses that are approved within its sphere. After that, a debate is held in the chamber, followed by decisions on the proposals from each committee (i.e., twenty-seven decisions in all). The budget as such is not approved until then. Finally, the Committee on Finance will examine all estimates and coordinate the national budget (see the Riksdag Act Chapter 4, Article 6, section 2 of supplementary provision 2). In the fall of 2013, the opposition parties joined their forces and thus managed to stop a tax reduction proposed by the government. This move was generally seen as contrary to earlier practice in this field. It remains to be seen whether future opposition parties will use the rules in the same way.

119. From a principled perspective, it seems clear that the reform has brought about a strengthening of a minority government, which is above all a result of the new requirement that votes will take place on all different areas of expenditure, after which the total budget is agreed upon. This means that it will now be much more difficult for majorities, who may agree on some of those posts but not all, to go against the budget proposed by the Government, unless they can agree on the whole budget between themselves. The reform was a consequence of the severe economic crisis in the early 1990s and is generally considered as instrumental in solving those problems. At the same time, it must be noted that it has further limited popular sovereignty, in line with many other, simultaneous Constitutional developments, since it in fact means that the majority of the Parliament is not any more, at least not always, in a position to secure or push through its will concerning the elaboration and content of such an important decision as the budget.

53. See the Riksdag Act Ch. 5, Art. 12. It may be noted that Ch. 5, Art. 12, supplementary provision 1 enumerates the different sectors of expenditure, the handling of which are divided between all the committees of the Parliament except the Law Committee (*Lagutskottet*).

§4. Delegation and Distribution of Legislative Power: Relation to the European Union

I. Background and General Remarks

120. The rules concerning delegation of legislative power in Chapter 8 IG, which are as mentioned indeed quite complicated, have been discussed above in Part I. As is generally known, Sweden joined the EU together with Finland and Austria on 1 January 1995. This means that there is now also another kind of delegation or distribution to focus upon, namely the delegation upwards from the Swedish Parliament, to the EU. This important issue also needs to be analysed here.

121. The membership found its legal (and political) support in an accession treaty concluded in February 1994 and a referendum on 13 November 1994, in which 52.4% voted yes and 46.7% no. (82% of the registered voters participated in this referendum and it may be noted that only Swedish citizens were allowed to vote, as a contrast to ordinary parliamentary elections.)[54]

122. After the referendum had taken place, the Constitutional changes described below were enacted. Those rules in Chapter 10, Article 5 IG were applied for the first time when the Amsterdam Treaty was ratified in 1998, but were for certain reasons still not considered to be totally updated, which led to some minor but nonetheless important changes in 2002, after ratification also of the Nice Treaty, as will also be explained below. Another important event, the legal basis of which was very doubtful and whose background was indeed very peculiar, was the referendum on membership within the Economic and Monetary Union (EMU) in 2003, which will also be roughly dealt with.

123. As a background to subsequent EU discussions, it may be noted that nationalism in Sweden has tended, at least after democratization some eighty years ago, to be less bragging and less about flag-waving and parades on the national holiday than in many other, also Nordic states. Instead, in a deeply collectivistic country, Swedes have been proud of things like the fine welfare system and the tradition of peaceful neutrality. The discussions on the nature and content of Swedish nationalism have increased recently, due to the great success of the nationalist party in the elections in 2014.

124. It is against this background that the effects of the economic crisis in the early 1990s should be seen. Suddenly, Sweden was no longer a model for the rest of the world, but rather a symbol of a kind of societal model that no longer worked and was in need of a profound change. Now, the somewhat strange aspect of this development was that the initial response to the crisis by the Swedish population, in the aftermath of the events of 1989, was to be strongly in favour of joining the EU. At that point, membership of the EU was perceived as a first, necessary step towards renewed economic prosperity. Gradually, however, from 1992 until early 1994, this

---

54. It may also be noted that invalid or blank votes are simply not included in the calculation.

opinion was going to change and the Union was instead going to be seen as a mortal threat to the Swedish welfare state.

125. How did this change in opinion come about, then? As indicated above, the conservative government in power from 1991 to 1994 was strongly pro-European. Though initially supported in this view by the electorate that had brought it to power, the government probably made a big mistake by starting to explain necessary but painful economic cutbacks by the need to prepare the country for EU membership. Instead of gaining respect and understanding for its tough measures, that government and thereby also the EU were seen as undermining a traditional societal model which most of the voters in fact wanted back, since they felt that it represented wealth and stability.

126. This situation could be seen as mainly resulting from a lack of communication, in that case. But the issue was in fact a little bit more complicated than that.

127. One of the main characteristics of Sweden as a state today, which distinguishes it from any other western democratic society (in fact, the only equivalent here seems to be Mexico), is, as mentioned above in the beginning of Part II, the fact that one-party, the Social Democrats, has held governmental power almost without interruption since 1932.[55] In order to understand why Sweden finally voted in favour of joining the EU in November 1994 (52.3%), after Austria and Finland had both voted in favour,[56] it is vital to keep in mind the return to power of the Social Democrats in September of that same year, 1994. Most right-of-centre voters were likely to be in favour of the EU anyway, but in order to convince the number of labour voters necessary for an affirmative result in the referendum, it was probably necessary to have the Social Democrats back in office (which is of course not a political statement, but only an objective, if perhaps somewhat cynical, analysis). Once back in government, the Social Democrats could argue that they were going to restore the welfare state and that the membership in the EU was one of the measures necessary to accomplish this. Without managing to convince the whole party, which for a long time used to be very sceptical of the European integration, embracing its own traditions of neutrality and the welfare state, and which did in fact come out of the campaign deeply split, a sufficient number of voters obviously believed the arguments. And the firm belief that EU membership was in fact good for Swedish economy and would give Sweden greater influence in the EU was shared by all the major parties.

128. If you analyse this debate a little more closely and compare it for instance with Denmark, it may be noted that the idea of the EU as a political instrument was not at all neglected or rejected. On the contrary, the EU was now described as a

55. The only exceptions until 2006 were the periods 1976–1982 and 1991–1994, when conservative or right-wing governments were in fact not very successful in trying to introduce their policies.
56. For a comparison with those two countries, and their respective reasons to join the EU, I may refer to my Article Reasons Why a Small Country Would Want to Become a Member of the European Union (Taking the Nordic Countries as Examples), in European Integration: History and Perspectives, Lausanne (Institut Suisse de Droit Comparé, vol. 45) 2002, pp. 65–76.

political means to balance the power of global capitalism. At the same time, however, sensitive issues like supranationalism were avoided as far as possible, which may be understandable if you want the approval of the voters in one of Europe's oldest nation states. Whatever you may think of that debate, it gave a more realistic image of what membership in the EU would mean than has ever been seen for instance in Denmark, as well as in a few other Member States. It is also likely that November 1994, with the Social Democrats back in power after three rather hard years with a conservative government, and after Austria and Finland had already decided to join, was in fact one of the few moments in modern history when a majority of normally Euro sceptic Swedes were prepared to vote 'yes' to joining the Union.[57]

129. Still, this did not mean that the problems, or the ambivalence in the Swedish opinion had disappeared.

130. Since the Social Democrats have always concentrated on staying in power, the first thing they had to focus on after the referendum was to heal the wounds in the party. This explains the obvious lack of interest that the Swedish government displayed in the development of EU affairs – and the general absence of debate on those issues – between 1994 and 1999, when the government finally started to be a bit more active. It also explains the decision, made already in 1997, not to join the third phase of the EMU, since the party strategists had decided that such a step would have made electoral victory in 1998 impossible. Thus, future decisions on Swedish participation in various fields of EU activities will probably always be made in light of what is beneficial for the Social Democratic Party, probably one of the most efficient political power machines in the world. This is undoubtedly most likely to make Sweden an unreliable partner and EU member also in the future, at least as long as the domestic political scene is not changed more profoundly than just by a change of government.

131. From this point of view, it is slightly surprising, then, that the rest of the EU Member States, and the European Commission, have accepted Sweden's decision not to join the EMU for the time being, despite the fact that Sweden cannot point to a legally valid exception which permits it to stay outside EMU should it so wish (as opposed to Denmark and United Kingdom, who both benefit from such exceptions).The new Article 139 of the Treaty on the functioning of the EU (TFEU) has undoubtedly facilitated Sweden's position.

132. From a strictly internal, national perspective, however, the biggest flaw in developments after the referendum of 1994, apart from the unhappy referendum on the euro in September 2003, which will be discussed further below, is probably the total absence of any debate on the rather vital issue of identifying the main purpose and ambitions of Sweden's membership. In particular, when you consider that the argument of having political influence in Europe was one of the main reasons for

57. Although it should be noted that since 2005, a majority of Swedes regularly support the EU Membership as such in opinion polls.

joining the Union, it is strange that Sweden has acted as a reluctant EU Member ever since 1 January 1995, both in relation to the other Member States and internally, where the tendencies of average voters to blame the EU for everything that is bad, has not been met with any constructive dialogue or debate by political bodies. Not even during the Swedish presidency of the EU in the first half of 2001 did this change, despite certain efforts of the government.

133. Against this background, the new rule in Chapter 1, Article 10 is in any case a certain indication of the fact that Swedish politicians do now want to look forward as far as the relationship with the EU is concerned. Also the rather unproblematic and successful presidency of the EU in the second half of 2009 may have contributed to this.

II. The European Issue in Chapter 10 of the Instrument of Government

134. The Constitutional regulation covering EU membership as well as other kinds of international agreements, is to be found in Chapter 10, Article 6 of the Instrument of Government (IG), the main Constitutional act. A few words could be said about the historical background for this regulation, which today reads as follows:

> Within the framework of European Union cooperation, the Riksdag (Parliament) may transfer a right of decision-making which does not affect the principles of the form of government. Such transfer presupposes that the protection for rights and freedoms within the field of cooperation to which the transfer relates corresponds to that afforded under this Instrument of Government and the European Convention for the Protection of Human Rights and Fundamental Freedoms.
> The Riksdag approves such transfer by means of a decision in which at least three fourths of those voting and more than half of the Members of Parliament concur. The Riksdag's decision may also be taken in accordance with the procedure prescribed for the enactment of fundamental law. Transfer cannot be approved until after the Riksdag has approved the agreement under Article 3.
> Of importance here is also Chapter 10, Articles 7-8:
> Article 7: A right of decision-making which is directly based on the present Instrument of Government and which purports at the laying down of provisions, the use of assets of the State or the conclusion or denunciation of an international agreement or obligation, may in other cases be transferred, to a limited extent, to an international organization for peaceful cooperation of which Sweden is a member, or is about to become a member, or to an international court of law. No right of decision-making relating to matters concerning the enactment, amendment or abrogation of fundamental law, the Riksdag Act or a law on elections for the Riksdag, or relating to the restriction of any of the rights and freedoms referred to in Chapter 2 may be thus transferred. The provisions laid down for the enactment of fundamental law apply in respect of

a decision relating to such transfer. If time does not permit a decision in accordance with these provisions, the Riksdag may approve transfer by means of a decision in which at least five sixths of those voting and at least three fourths of members concur.
If it has been laid down in law that an international agreement shall have validity as Swedish law, the Riksdag may prescribe, by means of a decision taken in accordance with the procedure laid down in paragraph two, that also any future amendment of the agreement binding upon the Realm shall apply within the Realm. Such a decision shall relate only to a future amendment of limited extent.
Article 8: Any judicial or administrative function not directly based on this Instrument of Government may be transferred, in a case other than a case under Article 6, to another state, international organization, or foreign or international institution or community by means of a decision of the Riksdag. The Riksdag may also in law authorize the Government or other public authority to approve such transfer of functions in particular cases.
Where the function concerned involves the exercise of public authority, Riksdag approval shall take the form of a decision in which at least three fourths of those voting concur.

135. Roughly speaking, Article 6 was introduced when Sweden joined the EU in 1995, while Articles 7–8 date back to the enactment of the new Constitution in 1974 or even before that.[58] Already in 1964, the possibility to transfer decision-making powers to an international organization aiming at peaceful cooperation was established, although this could then only take place to a limited extent. Though those provisions could of course not be used in order to facilitate an EU membership, this Constitutional reform was thus actually enacted as early as forty years ago, with the future relation to the European Community in mind (given that Sweden had applied for an association to the union already in 1961). Those new rules were then transferred to the new Constitution in 1974, adding only that transfer of competencies could also take place to an international court.[59] On both occasions, there was political unanimity on the introduction of the new Constitutional provisions, which only the former Communist Party (today left party) opposed.

136. However, if the pure text is to be analysed further, it may be said that Articles 7–8 permit transfers of legislative powers, budgetary powers including the use of the assets of the state and the treaty-making power, all to a limited extent, to *other* international organizations than the EU, while the possibility to transfer rights of decision-making to the EU itself is, and has ever since 1995 been much wider and more general. From a material point of view, such a transfer is limited only by the standard of the protection of human rights within the EU.

58. A useful comment on the historical background of this Article, and its history 'before 1995', is made by Karl-Göran Algotsson, Sveriges författning efter EU-anslutningen, Stockholm 2000 (SNS), p. 273 s. See also E. Holmberg/N. Stjernquist, Vår författning, 13th ed. Stockholm 2003 (edited by M. Isberg/G. Regner).
59. Some minor changes were also introduced in 1976 and 1985; see Algotsson, *supra*, p. 274.

137. From what has been said above, it follows that when Sweden was going to join the EU, the question was if those two articles, which were then the three last sections of Chapter 10, Article 5, would be sufficient or not. In other words, was a Constitutional reform required or not in order to enable Sweden to join the EU?

138. The first committee that attempted to deal with that question, the so-called Constitutional committee for joining the EC (*Grundlagsutredningen inför* EG, SOU (*Statens offentliga utredningar*, Official Bills and Proposals) 1993:14), answered it in the affirmative but proposed a new Chapter 1, Article 10, according to which the supremacy of any kind of EC law in relation to any Swedish law, including the Constitution, should be clearly stated or declared. However, the criticism against that proposal was very heavy in the spring of 1993, mainly due to political reasons; it was seen as a sign of Swedish resign or capitulation before Europe and was identified with an unlimited handling over of power to Brussels.[60] Consequently, the government quickly proposed three other alternatives,[61] one of which was similar to the one finally chosen. However, it must be noted that this solution was very much influenced by certain jurisprudence from the German Constitutional Court, Bundesverfassungsgericht (BVerfG).

139. The background to this is that according to Chapter 8, Article 14 of the Act of Government, Constitutional changes must as mentioned above in Part I be presented in Parliament nine months before a general election (and then approved, by a simply majority of the members of Parliament, in two subsequent and identical decisions before and after the election). Such an election was going to take place in September 1994 and it was later, in February 1994, also decided that the referendum on EU membership should be held in November that same year. Thus, the proposal for Constitutional reform had to be presented to the Parliament in December 1993, at the latest, in order to facilitate EU membership (given that what is now Articles 7–8 of IG 10:5[62] was not enough to fulfil this) and, further, this proposal had, from the point of view of the government, to have another content or at least form than the first, unpopular proposal, which was seen as a kind of a gift to the already very strong no-side in the forthcoming referendum.

140. Compared with the earlier text, the main changes in the new proposal were that the former requirement that transfer of competencies could only occur to a limited extent was abolished and, above all, that the previous mentioning of transfers, in general, to an 'international organization for peaceful cooperation' was replaced by a specific mentioning of transfer of decision-making powers to the three European Communities (which was only in 2002 changed to the EU). But this transfer could only take place under the condition (or, as it read, 'as long as', 'så länge' (cfr *Solange*, as in the so-called Solange judgments from the German Constitutional

60. For a further analysis of this debate, see Algotsson, *supra*, p. 275 ss as well as Ulf Bernitz, Sverige och Europarätten, Stockholm 2002, p. 109 ss and M. Melin/G. Schäder (who were both members of this legislative committee), EU:s konstitution, 6th ed., Stockholm 2003 p.
61. Which were all presented in the report Ds 1993:36, Våra grundlagar och EG – förslag till alternativ.
62. That is the former ss 1–3.

Court))[63] that the protection of fundamental rights within those Communities was as far-reaching as the one envisaged by the 2nd Chapter of the IG (dealing with basic human rights) and the European Convention for the Protection of Human Rights and Fundamental Freedoms.[64]

141. Here, the influence of the case law of the German Constitutional Court seems clear. It seems evident that the governmental committee analysing the Constitutional conditions for a future EU membership, facing itself in severe time pressure since it was necessary, due to Constitutional requirements, to present a proposal no later than in the middle of December 1993, more or less by chance stumbled upon the Maastricht judgment of BVerfG on 12 October 1993,[65] which somehow seemed to indicate a solution to the Swedish dilemma since it conditioned further transfer of decision-making power on the future development within the EU. Then, the committee also discovered the two Solange judgments from 1974 and 1986, the language of which thus found its way into the Swedish Constitution. In other words, the position of BVerfG suddenly was also the one chosen by the Swedish Constitutional legislator.

142. Also this formulation based on the Solange doctrine ('as long as') was changed in 2002, giving way, as seen above, to the rather vague notion of 'the principles of the form of government'.[66] Nevertheless, the basic content of this Chapter 10, Article 6 (former first section of IG 10:5) is still the same. So what does this Article really mean, then?

143. First of all, this is above all a rule to be used when new treaties are agreed upon. It has been used in relation to the ratification of the Amsterdam and Nice treaties and is likely to be used for a possible or an eventual ratification of the new Constitution for Europe, upon which Sweden is not likely to hold a referendum. Thus, it made it possible for Sweden to join the EU once the referendum in November 1994 had resulted in a positive yes vote, but it has also made it possible for Sweden to ratify new treaty changes, in an actually not very complicated manner, since the only material requirement for this to take place is that the protection of basic human rights within the EU will continue to be reasonably high (which has, as we know, not been a problem this far). The reasons given in the bill preparing this reform for choosing this particular solution were that it will mean that Sweden will not in the future be bound to accept the legal situation that existed at the time of joining the EU *and* that the legal acts of the Union could otherwise not be questioned in Swedish domestic law by using national rules on the protection of basic rights.

63. Entscheidungen des Bundesverfassungsgerichts (BVerfGE) 37, 271 and 73, 339.

64. This means, then, that those two catalogues of basic human rights (or 'Grundrechte') should be read together, in order to analyse if the protection within EU law corresponds to their added value of protection of basic human rights. However, the two catalogues are mutually over-lapping, albeit with some differences. In reality, if the question would ever become a real problem, the measurement of the applicable human rights standard could turn out to be quite tricky.

65. The so-called *Brunner* or *Maastricht* case, BVerfGE 89, 155.

66. A proposal based on the governmental bill SOU 2001:19.

144. According to this line of reasoning, which shows clear traces from arguments used not only by the German Constitutional Court in its Maastricht judgment from 1993, but also by the Danish Supreme Court in a similar judgment in 1998,[67] legal acts from the EU that fall outside the area where a transfer of sovereignty has taken place (i.e., outside the areas where the Union or the European Community is competent to act, cfr Article 3 of the EC Treaty) are on the other hand *ultra vires* and thus not applicable within the domestic legal system or by the national courts, who may simply set them aside. This may in fact be too simplified; the main problem with that line of reasoning is, of course, that according to the settled jurisprudence of the European Court of Justice (ECJ), only that court has the competence to decide whether a certain EU act is in fact invalid (because it is *ultra vires* or due to other reasons).[68] Here, national courts and authorities in quite a few Member States seem not to agree with ECJ, quite simply.

145. A few words should also be said about the formal requirements for a transfer of decision-making powers to the EU. Such a transfer by one single decision of the Riksdag will thus require a majority of 75% *of the voting* members; the alternative is that it will take place in the same way as a change of the Constitution, i.e., through two identical decisions, one before and one after a general election (cfr Chapter 8, Article 14).[69] It may be noted that while the public Swedish opinion has so far been regrettably hostile to the EU membership, as shown most clearly in the controversial referendum on the euro in September 2003, parties who are in favour of the membership have had a solid majority within the Parliament, holding more than 80% of the places there all the time since 1994 (and even before). This also means that the decisions on transfer of decision-making powers that have been made so far, in 1994, 1998 (Amsterdam) 2001 (Nice) and 2008 (Lisbon) have all taken place through one single decision, with the necessary majority.[70] (The one in 1994 did not even require qualified majority, due to a specific transfer rule which in a way implemented the result of the referendum that year directly; as stated above, this illustrates that Chapter 10, Article 6 is above all, and has from the beginning been considered mainly as a rule concerning ratification of new treaties or treaty changes.)

146. From a theoretical point of view, this kind of regulation makes it possible for Sweden to adhere to new treaties or treaty changes without having to change the Constitution, which is a practical advantage. Also the process for ratification as such

67. U 1998.800 H.
68. See for example the well-known case *Foto-Frost*, 314/85, ECR 1987, p. 4199.
69. As follows from Ch. 10, Arts 7–8, this could actually also lead to a referendum on the issue, should one-third of the members of the Parliament so wish. So far, however, this possibility to hold a referendum on a Constitutional change has never been used, but should parties who oppose the EU come to hold a sufficient number of seats (i.e., 117), it seems almost certain that this will come to happen.
70. A question to be asked in that respect is whether there may be any material differences between what may be transferred to the EU using one or the other of the two procedures. Personally, I do not think that neither the wording of IG 10:6–8, nor the practical experience during ten years of membership point towards any such difference, but the issue has been raised in the doctrine (e.g., by Holmberg/Stjernquist, *supra*, p. 199 s.).

is uncomplicated, not least compared with the requirements in many other Member States. At the same time, it may be noted that the Constitution does not at all mention the fact that Sweden *is* a member of the EU, despite all the preparations made in order to make membership possible.[71] This may be seen as yet another sign of the rather weak European commitment in Sweden, also in leading political circles.

147. The reference to the level of the protection of basic rights within EC law is interesting, since this is something which has never before been so clearly identified as an important aspect of the Swedish Constitution. Traditionally, the national protection of basic rights is also rather weak in Sweden, where there is no Constitutional court and not even a strong tradition of judicial review by the ordinary courts. Once again, the influence of German Constitutional jurisprudence, 'discovered' by the Constitutional legislators at a particular, crucial moment may be stressed. Furthermore, since the protection of basic rights within EU has grown stronger since 1994, as mentioned before, it seems clear that Sweden may continue to transfer decision-making powers to the EU.

148. Regardless of what has been said above, the question must be asked: As long as the transfer of decision-making power to the EU has taken place in the formally correct way and the Union is not acting *ultra vires*, which rules do then apply in Sweden? In other words, which is the view of the Swedish Constitution and its *travaux préparatoires* on the issue of supremacy of EC law?

149. Oddly enough, as it may seem, this issue is not mentioned anywhere in those acts, which may primarily be explained by the hostile reactions against the proposal from the first committee working on those issues, as mentioned above. Still, this has not prevented Swedish courts from acknowledging the supremacy of EC law in some important cases. However, since the legal support for the supremacy principle cannot be found in Chapter 10, Articles 6–8 of the national Constitution, it must instead be gathered from general principles of EC law, which was also what the Supreme Administrative Court did in an important case in 1997.[72]

150. As said before, the Article in question has been applied three times. In a law proposal from 1998 (1997/98:58), the government proposed that Sweden should ratify the Amsterdam Treaty, which was then formally done in two steps. First, the law regulating Sweden's accession (1994:1500), which enumerates a number of legal acts that are valid in Sweden since the 1 January 1995, was added in order to include the new treaty as such and a Swedish declaration accepting the widened jurisdiction of the ECJ. Second and more important, the Riksdag voted in favour of accepting the Treaty in a vote on 29 April 1998, with only some forty no-votes. Three years later, in 2001, the Nice Treaty was ratified in the same way, and the same thing happened in 2008 with the Lisbon Treaty, which all shows that the

71. For criticism against this fact, see Bernitz, *supra*, p. 110 s.
72. Case *Lassagård, Regeringsrättens Årsbok* (RÅ) 1997 ref. 65.

former Chapter 10, Article 5 worked very smoothly, as intended – at least as long as the solid majority of the Parliament is in favour of EU membership.

151. The two main changes of the rule that occurred in 2002 were the above-*mentioned* reforms in Chapter 10, Article 5, section 1, today to be found in Chapter 10, Article 6, according to which decision-making power may be transferred not as before to the European Communities, but to the EU instead and that such a transfer presupposes not only that the protection of rights and freedoms within the EU corresponds to the European Convention and the second Chapter of the Instrument of Government, but also that it 'does not affect the principles of the form of government'. It may of course be asked what this latter formulation really means and the *travaux préparatoires* are in fact not very clear on this point. The expression is indeed very vague. It seems, however, to refer to the discussion by the Constitutional committee in 1994, referred to above, and could perhaps be seen as an attempt to codify that discussion (with whatever effect that may have). As for the other change, which makes it possible to transfer decision-making powers to the EU instead of to the three communities, that seems to be logical given that the EU has since 1994 increased its powers and competencies in the so-called second and third pillars considerably (and is in the new Constitutional proposal even given a legal personality of its own).

152. Apart from that, a further change has occurred in Chapter 10, Article 2, according to which since 2003 the Government may not conclude any binding international agreement without approval of the Parliament, if the agreement presupposes the amendment or abrogation of an act of law or the enactment of a new act of law, or if it otherwise concerns a matter which it is for the Riksdag to determine. This rule, which was enacted after the approval of the Nice treaty, applies also to new EU treaties, which means that in the future new EU treaties – like the EU Constitution – must be approved twice, so to speak; first, the Parliament must approve the agreement as such, with three fourths majority or by two decisions with an election in between according to Chapter 10, Article 3, section 2, and then a new, separate decision must be made, with the same formal requirements, concerning the transfer of power to the EU that the new or amended treaty will entail. Undoubtedly, this is an important change, the effects of which remain to be seen.

153. Another change that should be mentioned here is to be found in Chapter 10, Article 10, according to which the Government shall keep the Riksdag continuously informed and confer with bodies appointed by the Riksdag concerning developments within the framework of EU cooperation. In practice, this is done through regular information from ministers to a specific parliamentary committee, the so-called *EU-nämnden*. More detailed regulations on how this information shall take place is to be found in Chapter 10 of the Riksdag Act, where a number of new rules strengthening the powers of the Parliament were introduced in 2009.

III. The EMU Issue

154. When Sweden joined the EU in 1995, the original decision to transfer decision-making powers to the union was based on and included the legal situation, and all the legal acts, existing at that moment; *l'acquis communautaire*, in one word. No exception was made as far as participation in the European Monetary Union was concerned, including its third step. The rules concerning the EMU in the EC Treaty did of course already exist at that time, though the common currency was not yet a reality. From that point of view, the Swedish legal situation was very similar to or in fact even identical with the situation of Austria and Finland, who joined the EU at the same time and who are today full EMU members. Still, Sweden later decided to have a new, special referendum on EMU, which in September 2003 resulted in a rather massive no vote (57% of the voters, representing 80% of the electorate). How was this development possible? Was it even legal?

155. The first question is the easiest one to answer, since the reason for this peculiar Swedish deviation from its obligations as an EU member simply has to do with domestic politics. After the referendum in 1994, only the two no-parties, Environmentalists and (former) Communists, together with the small farmers party, who had been in favour of EU membership but opposed the idea of a common currency, demanded a new referendum on this topic. Thus, the huge parliamentary majority was against such an idea. However, when returning to Swedish domestic politics in the fall of 1997, having acted for two years as a UN peace broker in Bosnia, right-wing opposition leader and former prime minister, Carl Bildt, in a surprising move during a parliamentary debate, in the build-up to the 1998 parliamentary election, called for a referendum to be held on this special topic.[73] Since he had at that time already consulted the liberals and the Christian Democrats, only the governing Social Democrats (with 45% of the seats in Parliament) did at that time not formally support the idea of a new referendum, which meant that this became a political reality or even necessity. It may also be added that the Social Democrats did never formally oppose the idea, which was logical given the internal division within the party over this issue. Thus, no political party or force, including the media, really ever opposed the idea of organizing this referendum, at least not on legal grounds. The very simple legal fact that the membership and the result of the referendum in 1994 did not allow this second referendum has never really been invoked in the Swedish debate, which is after all slightly surprising.

156. From the legal point of view, it is, to my view, in reality clear that Sweden has already since 1997, when the original decision was made not to participate in the third step of EMU, violated its obligations as an EU member. Sweden thus became the first country to meet the so-called convergence criteria but still not participate in the EMU, without any legally binding exception that enables it to remain outside (of the kind that both Denmark and the UK have since 1991).

---

73. It may be noted that since October 2006, Mr Bildt is Foreign Minister and that his role in the EMU debacle has actually been surprisingly little discussed in Sweden.

157. Formally, however, this has not quite been the official truth. Instead, the Swedish non-participation in EMU has been explained, e.g., by the EU Commission in a report dated 25 March 1998, by the fact that Sweden has remained outside ERM, the so-called Exchange Rate Mechanism; formally, adherence to that system for two years is a necessary but not sufficient condition for participation in the third step of EMU. But if this is to be taken into account, it must be noted that Sweden has decided not to take part in ERM autonomously. EU has thus never decided to keep Sweden outside that system.

158. As it turned out, 57% of the voters voted against the euro on 14 September 2003, only three days after the assassination of Foreign Minister Anna Lindh. It may of course be asked if that turnout might have been different, had the government spent more time and energy arguing in favour of the common EU currency already in 1999 or 2000. What is more important, however, is to analyse the legal situation that this no vote has led to. In that respect, it should be noted that Sweden has not, not even after the referendum, asked for a formal exception from the obligation to participate in the EMU, which means that the original legal obligation to work for and try to achieve a full Swedish membership in the monetary union still remains, though very little has been said on this topic in the Swedish political debate in the last year. While it may be understood that the Swedish political establishment does not want to return to this topic immediately after the terrible days surrounding the huge failure in the referendum, this means that the EMU question will continue to haunt Sweden for the foreseeable future. The official version is that the time for a new referendum will not occur until 2010, at the earliest, but is it even then a good idea at all to organize a new referendum on the topic? Does that not in reality mean endowing the referendum of 2003 with a formal legitimacy that it has in fact never possessed, as explained above? And what would happen if a new referendum in 2010 or later would once again lead to a negative result? How would that affect Sweden's long time position within the EU? How will the situation be affected by the entrance into EMU of new Member States?

159. This legally highly unclear situation – which has perhaps been made a little easier due to the new Article 139 of the Treaty on the Functioning of the EU, which formally includes Sweden among the EU Member States with exceptions from the euro – is all the more regrettable since the other Constitutional preparations for a membership of the EMU were conducted or implemented already in 1998/99, in accordance with the provisions of Chapter 8, Article 15.[74] Basically, those consist of changes in Chapter 9, regulating the financial power of the realm, Articles 12 and 13. According to those rules, the Government is responsible for general currency policy matters, while the Riksbank, the central bank of the Realm, working under the Parliament and thus formally independent from the government, is responsible for monetary policy. No public authority may determine how the Riksbank shall

74. It may also be noted, in this respect, that Sweden actually conducted a severe economic policy, characterized by austerity, in 1994–1996. This was explicitly made above all in order to meet the so-called convergence criteria necessary for an EMU membership, which makes the subsequent development even less logical and harder to understand.

decide in matters of monetary policy. The eleven members of the governing council of the Riksbank are all appointed by the Riksdag, who also considers whether the members of the Governing Council or the Executive Board of the bank shall be granted discharge of responsibility. A member of the Executive Board may be removed from office only if he no longer fulfils the requirements laid down for performing his duties or if he has been guilty of gross negligence. All those rules, aimed at ensuring the independence of the Riksbank, meet the criteria laid down in the EC Treaty for enabling Member States to join the EMU. A future Swedish EMU membership will thus be easy to obtain from a strict legal point of view, but probably not when all the political aspects are taken into account.[75]

IV. Conclusions

160. From the reading above, it seems clear that the Swedish Constitutional regulation of its EU membership is pragmatic, in terms of making it possible for the country to adhere to new treaty changes. The events surrounding the referendum on the euro and its roots in domestic political/tactical aspects also show that the leading politicians, in all parties, share a tendency not to consider the legal implications of EU membership, i.e., its obligations very seriously. Given the somewhat isolated and independent history of the country, this rather weak European commitment is perhaps not entirely surprising.

161. More recently, the meaning or significance of the new wording of IG 10:6 and of the words 'principles of the form of government' in particular has been discussed in relation to the (later abandoned) Draft EU Constitution, which contained, as may be generally known, a rule (Article I-6) according to which EC law in general (i.e., the new Constitution 'and law adopted by the institutions of the Union in exercising competences conferred on it') 'shall have primacy over the law of the Member States'.

162. Thus, the national Constitutions were not mentioned here, which ought to mean, given the different views on the scope of the supremacy of EU law in relation to national law that is clear if you compare e.g., the position and jurisprudence of the ECJ with that of the German Constitutional Court, that no change would be likely to occur; in other words, the issue whether EU law has supremacy also over national Constitutions would continue to be unresolved. However, in a special Declaration to the Draft Constitution, (No. 1) the Member States, somewhat surprisingly, stated that this new rule 'reflects existing case law' from the ECJ. In other words, the view of the ECJ concerning the scope of the supremacy principle, and not the one advocated e.g., by the Bundesverfassungsgericht in Karlsruhe, would here be indirectly 'codified'.

75. The current government, in which the Farmers party oppose an EMU membership, has so far not taken any new initiatives in this area. For criticism against this and other aspects of the Swedish Government's handling of the situation, see Nergelius, En olaglig folkomröstning – Sverige och EMU, Stockholm 2008.

163. A general view in the Swedish debate on this issue seems to be that the formulation stating that only decision-making which does not affect the principles of the form of government may be transferred to the EU is badly suited for practical purposes, since this kind of transfer does in fact normally concern issues like democracy, rule of law, legislation and the role of the courts and other public authorities. As to the practical effect that the new provision may have, both in relation to the new Constitution and in the future, that simply remains to be seen.

164. This, though perhaps now only of academic interest, was the formal, legal and Constitutional background, then, to the discussion concerning the ratification of the EU Constitution, which took place mainly in 2005. A few more words could perhaps be said, on the other hand, about its political background.

165. Above all, it must be noted that the Swedish politicians in general and the big parties in particular did not, and do still not, wish to have a referendum concerning the Constitution. This is in particular due to the traumatic effects of the referendum concerning the euro in 2003; it is hardly surprising that the leading parties then did not want to have a new referendum on the proposed EU Constitution, given that it was not necessary from any constitutional points of view.

166. Instead, the Government declared in late 2004 that the Constitution was going to be ratified by use of the above-*mentioned* possibility to enter into agreements of this kind through one single decision, with support of three-quarters of the voting MP's. It then also in the beginning of 2005 proposed a bill concerning the ratification, in which the Constitution was described as not conflicting with the requirements of IG Chapter 10, Article 5 (now Article 6).[76] The four right-wing opposition parties supported that opinion and the pathway suggested and parliamentary treatment of this bill then started in the spring of 2005, but after the no-results in the referendas in France and Netherlands in May–June 2005, the Government unilaterally, without consulting other parties, decided to suspend the process for ratification of the Constitution. This decision was announced in June 2005, after a similar decision from the British Government. It was not met with any resistance from other political parties and has not led to any further, intensified discussion on the future fate of Sweden's possible ratification of the Constitution.

167. When the bill concerning the proposed ratification of the Constitution was presented, and even before that, the Green (Environmentalist) Party as well as the Left Wing Party opposed its ratification and urged for a referendum (the closer rules on which are to be found in IG Chapter 8, Article 16, sections 3–4). The legal argument for this was that the Constitution was not compatible with and requires changes within the Swedish Constitution, which seems however to be exaggerated. Since those two parties do anyway not possess one-quarter of the places in the Parliament (which consists of a total of 349 members), those objections were anyhow not of any great political significance. What is more noteworthy, however, is that

76. Ds 2004:52, it may also be mentioned that the so-called Law Council, checking the Constitutionality of proposed legislation, supported this view in an opinion from June 2005. KOLL.

there has then been no further discussion, not even in the spring of 2007, when no less than eighteen Member States including Finland have ratified the constitution, on whether and how Sweden intends to do with the future ratification. Sweden eagerly supported the calls for further 'reflection' on how to proceed with the Constitution, as suggested by the EU itself, but has refused to be more specific than that. The new government in October 2006 actually confirmed this position of inactivity.

168. However, when the Lisbon Treaty was finally due for ratification in November 2008, all the main parties agreed to this ratification, which once again made any discussions concerning referendum unnecessary.

§5. Working Procedures of the Parliament Concerning Legislation

169. As far as budget procedures are concerned, a few words on the working procedures of the Parliament have already been said. What is perhaps even more important, however, is the working procedure concerning and related to legislation, the main or most important part of the work of the Parliament.

170. The main, crucial term in order to understand how a certain issue or matter is being treated by the Parliament is, according to the official translation of the Constitutional texts, 'business' (*ärende*), though issue, matter or errand would probably be just as relevant. But anyway, the two most important kind of business handled by the Swedish Parliament are deriving either from governmental bills (*proposition*) or from initiatives from individual MP's (*motion*).[77] Apart from that, the parliamentary committees (*riksdagsutskott*) have a right of their own to take new initiatives, while public authorities, companies or individuals lack such a capacity and will thus have to rely on lobbying if they want to influence parliamentary matters, an activity the condition of which was discussed in the beginning of this part of the book.

171. Once an initiative – in either one of those forms – has been raised within the Parliament, a decision of some kind is likely to occur, although that is not absolutely sure since the Parliament may decide simply not to deal with an issue (which is however unusual). Of the various initiatives, the governmental bills are undoubtedly the most important ones, since they are likely to result in new legislation. In each parliamentary session (*riksmöte*), some 200 bills are passed from the Government to the Parliament, which means that it is evident that the MP's are very busy dealing with those, not least in the various committees. According to Chapter 3, Article 1 of the Riksdag Act, a government bill must always include the Government minutes in the matter, an account of the preparation of the matter and a motivation of the proposal, as well as the opinion of the Law Council (*Lagrådet*) or as it is officially called, the Council of Legislation, whenever such an opinion exists.

77. See IG Ch. 4, Art. 3.

172. The budget bill, which has a special position in Swedish parliamentary and political life, shall be submitted no later than 20 September, as mentioned above, with an exception for the years when an election has occurred.[78] Concerning the submission of other bills, the Government shall, according to Chapter 3, Article 5 of the Riksdag Act, time them so as to prevent an accumulation of business in the Parliament, which seems however to be a constant source of irritation for the Parliament, who is not happy with the work of the Government in this respect.[79] In sheer numbers, however, the matters introduced by individual MP's is far higher than the number of official law proposals. The time to submit such 'private members' motions', as they are officially called, the so-called '*allmän motionstid*', runs from the start of a parliamentary session and until fifteen days have passed from the submission of the Budget Bill (see the Riksdag Act Chapter 3, Articles 10–11). Apart from that, specific motions arising out of a Government bill or a written communication from the Government or from a report from a parliamentary body other than a committee may be introduced within fifteen days from the date when that document was notified to the chamber. However, such motions, which may according to Chapter 3, Article 9 not concern more than one single topic, do very rarely lead to any concrete results in terms of e.g., legislation; they may rather be seen as a means for individual MP's to show that they are active and try to raise their profiles in various issues.[80]

173. Chapter 4 of the Riksdag Act deals according to its title with 'Preparation of business',[81] which is another way of expressing that it regulates the work of the various parliamentary committees. The IG is rather silent on this point, and simply states in Chapter 4, Article 3 that the Riksdag elects committees from among its members in accordance with rules laid down in the Riksdag Act and that those shall include a Committee on the Constitution (*Konstitutionsutskottet, KU*) and a Committee on Finance (*Finansutskottet, FiU*). Thus, those two committees are Constitutionally regulated[82] and therefore enjoy a somewhat stronger position than the other ones, of which the Committee on Taxation (*Skatteutskottet, SkU*) is the only one mentioned in an ordinary provision of the Riksdag Act (Chapter 4, Articles 2 and 5). The other, currently twelve ones, which may thus be abolished by one single decision by the chamber,[83] are enumerated in Chapter 4, Article 2, supplementary provision 1 and all their respective areas of competence in Chapter 4, Article 6, supplementary provisions 1–15.

---

78. See the Riksdag Act Ch. 3, Art. 2, supplementary provision 1.
79. Cfr Algotsson, *supra*, p. 185.
80. Motions, as well as other initiatives, may according to Ch. 3, Art. 17 of the Riksdag Act be withdrawn until a committee report has been presented on the matter, which underlines the strong position of the committees (*utskott*) within the system.
81. Or, in Swedish, 'Ärendenas beredning'.
82. See also IG Ch. 2, Art. 12, Ch. 8, Art. 15 and Ch. 9, where they are given other specific purposes and competences.
83. From Ch. 4, Art. 2 of the Riksdag Act it also follows that the committees are appointed for each electoral period. Special committees may also be appointed during the electoral period in order to serve for the remainder of that period, which was the case in 1992 for a committee dealing with the EEA agreement.

174. In Chapter 4, Article 5 IG it is also mentioned that any matter raised by the Government or by an MP *shall* be prepared by a committee before it comes up for decision, unless the IG states otherwise. The same thing is stated in Chapter 4, Article 1 of the Riksdag Act. Thus, there seems to be no doubt that the position of the committees is indeed very strong, in particular in the Swedish political culture where minority governments have been so frequent and parliamentary compromises are thus often sought within the committees.

175. If any system is sought concerning the way in which the matters are divided between the different committees, this basically has to do with their 'subject area', as stated in Chapter 4, Article 6 of the Riksdag Act. However, a committee may transfer a matter to another committee if deemed necessary, provided that the latter committee consents. At any given time, any committee may according to Chapter 4, Article 8 provide another committee with an opportunity to deliver an opinion concerning a matter affecting that latter committee's area of competence.[84] Furthermore, any committee may reach an agreement with one or more other committees to prepare a matter jointly through deputies on a joint committee (Chapter 4, Article 8, section 3).

176. Every committee consists of an odd number of members which is not lower than fifteen and currently seventeen (Chapter 4, Article 3 of the Riksdag Act). Proportionality between the political parties is always aimed for.[85] According to Chapter 4, Article 9, the committees *shall* deliver reports on all matters which have been referred to them and which have not been withdrawn (cfr Chapter 3, Article 17). According to a new rule in Chapter 4, Article 8 IG, every committee shall follow and evaluate all parliamentary decisions within its area of responsibility.

177. The right of the committees to take initiatives of their own, which is mentioned in Chapter 3, Article 7, is in fact very scarcely used.[86] What is more important from a practical point of view is the right for a minority of five committee members, under Chapter 4, Article 11 to urge the committee to obtain information or an opinion from any State Authority (*myndighet*). This applies to the Government only to a limited extent, but is important not least because it applies to the Law Council, though that fact hardly follows from the text, since that Council is not a typical State authority. In this way, a minority protection that vaguely resembles the system connected with *Conseil Constitutionnel* in France has been created, though the two systems are far from identical. What is also very important is the possibility for the committees, under Chapter 4, Article 13 to decide to hold public meetings. This possibility was created in 1988 and was almost immediately used for TV-sent, direct interrogations on the so-called *Ebbe Carlsson*-affair, which led to the resignation of the Minister of Justice. Normally, however, committee meetings take place

84. The special role of the Committee of Finance in this respect has been mentioned above in § 2.
85. Cfr Ch. 7, Art. 2, which expresses the same principle as far as the nomination committee of the Parliament (*Valberedningen*) is concerned.
86. With an exception for the general right to take such initiatives for the Committee of Finance, which was once again mentioned above in § 2.

behind closed doors, with an obligation for members and others present not to disclose what has been said (Chapter 4, Article 17). Still, voting within the committees shall be by open ballot, with a decisive vote for the chairman in the event of a tied vote (Chapter 4, Article 15).

178. That matter leads us over to how decisions are finally made in individual matters, or perhaps rather to the 'Settlement of business', as the headline of Chapter 5 of the Riksdag Act reads. That whole Chapter is in fact based on the assumption that matters initiated within the parliament shall be treated by different committees before returning to the chamber for a decision of some kind. The general rule in this respect is that a committee report shall be notified to the Chamber and then tabled twice there before decision; see Chapter 5, Articles 1–2 of the Riksdag Act, which includes a few exceptions from the main rule. The MP's may thus reflect upon the report before moving adoptions or rejections of its various proposals (Chapter 5, Article 3). The matter itself is then taken up for settlement once the Chamber has declared the debate closed, in response to a proposal from the Speaker and in accordance with Chapter 5, Article 4. It is then normally settled by acclamation or, if an MP so requests, by holding of a special vote. The settlement by acclamation is considerably less complicated, as follows from Chapter 5, Articles 5–7. In other cases, when a special vote is held, the Speaker has a considerable influence on the procedure and on which proposals that are put against each other, not least in the case of a tied vote (Article 7). In that case, a lottery may ultimately decide the outcome, although Swedish politicians have been trying to avoid lottery situations ever since the days of the equilibrium between the two blocks, with 175 MP's representing both sides, from 1973 to 1976. Now, when the Riksdag has 349 members, that ought not to be possible any more, but could still occur if some MP is absent or in similar situations.[87]

87. Concerning details in the voting rules, see Nergelius, *supra*, p. 69 ss.

Chapter 4. The Executive

§1. The Organ of State: Its Legal Status, Competences and Working Modes

179. The rules concerning the appointment and formation of the Government are to be found in Chapter 6 IG and are not very complicated as such. At the same time, however, they are related to and concern many principles which are of the utmost importance for the whole Swedish constitutional system, among which we must in particular note what is often referred to as "negative parliamentarianism". In short, that term means that a government must not necessarily enjoy the support of more than half of the MP's, as long as the majority of the MP's (i.e., 175) is not going to vote against it, as seen most recently in 2014. In many ways, this internationally unusual kind of parliamentary regulation may even be described as the core of modern Swedish parliamentarism, whatever we may think about it.

180. The other distinctive feature of modern Swedish constitutional regulation of parliamentary and political life, which may actually not be totally in line with what has been said above, is the regulation concerning the position of the Prime Minister, who does in fact enjoy a very strong position within the Government (which furthermore seems to be growing the whole time). According to Chapter 6, Article 1, the Government consists of the PM and other ministers and it is striking, when reading the rules concerning the appointment of the Government in Chapter 6, Articles 2–6 (and partly also its dischargement in Articles 7–9), that those do mainly and in the first part only concern the PM who, once elected, can freely pick the other ministers.[88] He (or she, although Sweden has so far never had a female PM) must, once approved, inform the Parliament as soon as possible about the names of the Ministers appointed, but the Parliament is then not in a position to oppose those appointments. Furthermore, the PM may according to Chapter 6, Article 8 at any particular moment when he wishes to do so discharge any other minister, which is a clear sign of the huge executive power that is vested in the hands of the PM. The number of ministers is not constitutionally regulated, though they must be at least five according to Chapter 7, Article 4.[89] From the ministers, the PM also appoints the heads of the various specific ministries (Chapter 7, Article 1). He also prescribes which matters or groups of matters that are to be presented by which ministers at the Government's meetings (Chapter 7, Article 5).

181. In fact, the Swedish constitution contains few, if any formal barriers to the powers of the PM. The government is formally to be considered as a body composed by the PM, whose members depend on his faith, belief, support and confidence in them. Still, it should be noted that the Government as a whole takes a collective responsibility for its decisions, which are reached at Government meetings (Chapter 7, Article 3). As a consequence, dissenting opinions must be published in the record from those meetings (Chapter 7, Article 6) and the dissenting

88. See in particular Ch. 6, Art. 4.
89. Traditionally, the Government consists of circa twenty ministers.

minister will then not share any formal or legal responsibility for that particular decision.

182. The constitutional dominance of the PM in relation to the other ministers is probably more evident in governments with only one-party than in coalition governments like the one in office since October 2006, where the PM has to cooperate with leaders of other parties, who in reality do of course exercise a decisive influence concerning which ministers that will represent their parties.[90] Apart from that particular situation, however, the PM is actually rather free to form the Government according to his own wishes. When doing so, he may as follows from Chapter 7, Article 8 IG also appoint a Deputy PM, who exercises or performs his duties in his absence.[91] If the PM has not appointed a deputy, or if the deputy is also absent, these duties are instead assumed by that minister among those currently in office who has been a minister for the longest time.[92]

183. Let us now look a little bit closer at how the PM and the Government is appointed and may possibly also be discharged. It is in fact here that the *negative parliamentarianism* works at its clearest.

184. First of all, it is clear that the rules in Chapter 6 will make it possible to form different kinds of governments, be they based on a majority of MP's or not. From 1973–1976, 1982–1991 and 1994–2006, Sweden was ruled by social democratic, one-party and minority governments. A coalition government supported by a majority of MP's were in power from 1976–1978 and 1979–1981 and again from October 2006–2010, while coalition and minority governments ruled from 1981–1982 and 1991–1994, as well as from 2010 and onwards. Finally, the absurd situation with a one-party (liberal) government, supported by 39 MP's and governing from October 1978–October 1979 must be mentioned once again, not least because it so clearly illustrates what may be described as an inherent weakness in the system.

185. The point of departure for the formation of a new government must always, in a parliamentary system like the Swedish one, be the number of mandates that the different parties hold in the parliament. A key role in the procedure for finding a new government is given to the Speaker of the Parliament. According to Chapter 6, Article 2 IG, when a PM is to be appointed, the Speaker summons for consultation representatives from each party group and confers with the Deputy Speakers before

90. Sometimes the ministers themselves do not seem to be aware of the content of those rules. Thus, when Liberal Party leader Mr Lars Leijonborg resigned as party leader in August 2007, he said that it was up to the new party leader Mr Björklund to decide whether he could stay on in the government, a statement that was obviously false from a constitutional point of view.
91. Since October 2006 until October 2010, the leader of the Farmers Party (Centerpartiet), Mrs Maud Olofsson, had that position. After the election in 2010, it went to the leader of the liberal party and Minister of Education Jan Björklund.
92. See IG Ch. 7, Art. 8, which also states that if two ministers in this peculiar situation should have served for equally long, the senior in age of them will have precedence.

placing a proposal before the Parliament, that shall then proceed to vote on the proposal no later than four days after that without prior preparation by any parliamentarian Committee. If more than half of the MP's (i.e., 175) vote against it, it is rejected, but otherwise, it is adopted. This means that it would be enough for one single MP, or even none at all, to vote in favour of the candidate, as long as not more than 174 vote against, which may be slightly surprising.[93]

186. Typically, this procedure does of course take place after a parliamentary election, but as shown not least in 1986, after the murder of the PM, or in 1996, when the PM resigned of his own free will, it is operational also in some other occasions. The same has happened when a coalition government has been replaced by another coalition government, with other parties but the same PM (1978 and 1991). This means, in other words, that the procedure for forming a new government is in reality a procedure for finding a new PM.

187. In this respect, a new rule in Chapter 6, Article 3, that did, however, not apply after the election in 2014, since the PM then resigned immediately, must be observed. According to this new rule, the newly elected Parliament must within two weeks after its reconvening vote on its confidence in the 'old' PM. This will thus make it impossible for the PM to simply 'stay on' in power, though it must be observed that the rule of 'negative parliamentarianism' mentioned above will apply also here. Thus, the old PM will be able to stay in power unless 175 MP's vote against him (or her). Should he choose to resign after the election, this new rule will of course not be used.

188. It should be noted, in that respect, that should the Parliament after all reject the Speaker's proposal for a new PM, the above-mentioned procedure is repeated (which has so far actually never happened, though). Should this, theoretically, happen four times, the procedure for appointing a PM is abandoned and resumed only after a parliamentary election has been held. In that case, if no ordinary election is due to be held within three months, an extraordinary election shall be held within that time, as follows from IG Chapter 6, Article 3.

189. Concerning the important role in this process of the Speaker, it could be noted that he or she is elected at the first meeting of the Chamber in the electoral period, *for that whole period*, according to Chapter 8, Article 1 of the Riksdag Act. Since the ordinary election will take place on the third Sunday of September and the Parliament will then not convene until fifteen days have passed, according to IG Chapter 3, Article 5, it is very likely that the old, retiring Speaker will be involved in the process, in particular if the election has led or looks likely to lead to a shift

93. The example is in fact not entirely theoretical, as was shown in the fall of 1978 when the liberal leader Ola Ullsten was elected as PM though being supported by only thirty-eight votes from his own party. Due to political considerations, the Social Democratic Party here did not vote at all. According to a comparative study by T. Bergman called simply Parlamentarism (which is to be found in I. Mattsson/O. Petersson (ed.), Svensk författningspolitik, Stockholm 2003 (SNS), pp. 130–147), Sweden and Portugal are the only countries in the Western world who have introduced such a clear model of negative parliamentarism.

of government. This was illustrated in the fall of 2014. Formally, however, the proposal for a new PM will not be put forward to the Chamber until a new speaker has been elected, which also means that the sitting Speaker will have the full formal responsibility for putting forward such a proposal when a new Prime Minister is to be elected in other situations than directly after an election (e.g., after the death or resignation of a former PM). In all those situations, we must expect that the Speaker has had consultations with the other Party groups and the Deputy Speakers, who normally represent other parties than his own (cfr IG Chapter 6, Article 2), before the proposal is made. So far, the rules have been working as expected, but certain tricky situations could be foreseen, for instance if a PM who has been accepted or tolerated by the Parliament (i.e., who has not received more than 174 votes against him) would then anyway refuse to accept the nomination, for instance because negotiations with other parties turned out to be more difficult than expected.[94] In order to avoid this, the Speaker, ever since a governmental crisis in 1978, has taken to the routine not only to propose a PM[95] but also to inform the Chamber about which kind of government that the proposed candidate intends to form. However, since the PM is totally free to appoint or discharge any minister as he likes, it seems to be impossible for the Speaker formally to bind the future PM through such statements.[96]

190. Once elected, however, the PM and the other ministers of the Government (cfr Chapter 6, Article 6) are not irremovable. According to Chapter 6, Article 7, should the Parliament actually declare that the PM or any other minister no longer enjoys its confidence, that minister will have to resign or formally, the Speaker will have to discharge him or her. And should the PM be discharged or die, the Speaker has to discharge also the other ministers according to Chapter 6, Article 9. A discharge of the PM is thus more dramatic than a discharge of any other minister.

191. This is of course a key element of the parliamentarian system. However, it must be noted that according to Chapter 6, Article 7 IG, if the Government is in a position to order an extraordinary election, no decision to discharge the minister in question should be announced (even if it should be the PM), provided that the Government will call for an extraordinary election within one week from the declaration of no-confidence. This has so far never happened and the votes on no-confidence that have until now taken place have in fact not had very dramatic consequences;[97] interestingly enough, the only time when a minister did resign in

---

94. Cfr Nergelius, *supra*, p. 48.
95. Which does, then, not mean that the Speaker formally instructs that person to form a government, but only that he suggests that the Parliament should approve the candidate to the post.
96. Cfr Nergelius, *supra* Formally, it would thus be possible for a PM to make use of his right to discharge ministers in order to change the composition of a coalition government, though it should be noted that when the formation of such governments was indeed changed in 1981, the government resigned and the PM was then reappointed. Furthermore, a PM who used his formal powers in that way, would be subject to huge criticism, not only from the affected parties but also from other parties, media and experts. For further historical background and examples, see Nergelius, *supra*, p. 49 ss.
97. For details, see Nergelius, *supra*, p. 52 ss.

such a situation was when the former Minister of Justice Ms Anna-Greta Leijon was facing such a vote of no-confidence in 1988, just a few months before ordinary elections (because of illegal involvement in private detective work related to the murder of former PM Olof Palme). Instead of facing the crisis, she preferred to resign in advance, since there seemed to be a majority of MP's supporting the vote against her.[98]

192. Should all the members of the Government have been discharged, they will according to Chapter 6, Article 11 remain at their posts until a new Government has assumed office. The same rule also states that if a minister other than the PM has been discharged at his own request, he remains anyway at his post until a successor has assumed office, should the PM so request.

193. There are also a few other, perhaps more formal, rules concerning the work of the Government that may be of interest. First of all, it should be noted that according to Chapter 6, Article 2, only a Swedish citizen may be a minister and that a minister may not have any other public or private employment, or be involved in any activity whatsoever which might impair public confidence in him.

194. The different ministries are organized under a common government office (*regeringskansli*), IG Chapter 7, Article 1.[99] Among the ministries, the Government itself allocates responsibilities and competences, something which is thus not constitutionally regulated but in fact quite often changed. In preparing Government business, the necessary information and opinions shall be obtained from the public authorities concerned, Chapter 7, Article 2. Organizations and private persons shall then be afforded an opportunity to express opinions as necessary, which is a part of the highly developed Swedish system of *preparing* legislation (which includes bills, presented in *utredningar*, which are then examined and commented upon by public authorities, NGO's and others who may have a vested interest in the case in a so-called *remissförfarande*).[100]

195. In fact, the IG regulates very little of the Government's work and hardly at all its details. The main rules, of a generally rather formal character, are to be found in Chapter 7 IG. Apart from that and apart from the rules concerning the election of the PM, rules on the Government's role and its competences in relation to the Parliament are to be found in different Chapters of the IG; its important role in the legislative and budgetary work has for instance already been discussed.

---

98. See also *further* below in Ch. 4, concerning among other things how a vote of no confidence is introduced in the Chamber.
99. There is also a special kind of influential Secretariat or 'ministry', though it is formally not a ministry, working directly under the PM, namely the so-called *Statsrådsberedningen*.
100. The bills from the Government presented to the Parliament are handed over as proposals, *propositioner*. Those are normally based on facts and findings presented in *SOU*, *Statens Offentliga Utredningar*, upon which the *remiss* comments are normally made. Points of view issued during the remiss procedure are often mentioned in the proposals. Minor, internal preparations of various matters, made by the ministries themselves, may also be presented in the so-called *Departementsserien* (*Ds*). Also those reports may be subject to a remiss procedure, though that is more unusual.

196. The important role and the very strong position of the PM has already been discussed. It should also be noted that according to Chapter 7, Article 4 IG, the PM summons other ministers to attend Government meetings and does also preside at such meetings (where at least five ministers must be present), though some Deputy PM may act in his absence in accordance with Chapter 7, Article 8.

197. A clear rule concerning the legal status and responsibility of ministers is to be found in Chapter 13, Article 3 IG, according to which a sitting or former minister may be held accountable for a criminal act committed in the performance of his ministerial duties only if he has thereby grossly neglected his official duties.[101] A decision to institute criminal proceedings against him (which has so far never happened) is then made by the Committee of the Constitution and the case will be tried before the Supreme Court. Surprisingly enough, the prosecution shall be brought before the Supreme Court by the well-known *Justitieombudsman*, JO.[102]

198. This provision is interesting and complicated from a few different points of view. First of all, it means that ministers may be prosecuted as individuals, although the Government is normally collectively responsible for its decisions, as explained above. Second, it may be discussed if the Constitutional Committee is under an obligation to decide that criminal proceedings shall be brought in such a situation as the one described here. Since the situation has until now never occurred, the issue may be theoretical, but it may of course be a problem that this Committee is politically composed, most likely with the governmental party or parties having a very strong influence there.[103] Finally, it must be noted that the Supreme Court may not, in the case of a criminal conviction against the minister, decide to separate him from his position, as opposed to a similar situation concerning an MP.[104] Instead, we must expect the PM in such a situation to dismiss that minister, though he is in fact not constitutionally obliged to do so (which once again shows the strong position of the PM).

---

101. It may of course be discussed what a gross neglect of the duties of a minister really means. Espionage seems to be a clear example, while severe crimes without any connection with the ministerial duties, like murder, theft or drug trafficking, would seem to fall outside the scope of this Article.
102. This does not follow from the IG but from a special statute with instructions to the Ombudsman. It is slightly surprising, since the control of the Government is in fact not one of his (or her, since the Ombudsman may despite the name be a woman) regular responsibilities. Generally speaking, the role of the Ombudsman (or ombudsmen, since there are now four of them, apart from ombudsmen for specific matters like discrimination on ethnical or gender basis) is much more limited and much less important today than it has been historically. According to Ch. 12, Art. 6 IG, an ombudsman is entitled to be present at the deliberations of a court of law or an administrative authority and shall therefore have access to its records and documents. A court of law or an administrative authority and any official working there, at state or local level, must always provide the Ombudsman with such information and opinions that he requests. The Ombudsman may also institute criminal or disciplinary proceedings against officials when there may be ground for that, but that function in particular has lost much of its importance in recent years.
103. See above in Ch. 3 concerning the work of the legislature and the composition of the various parliamentary committees.
104. Cfr IG Ch. 4, Art. 11, s. 3, discussed above in Ch. 3.

199. This rather tricky situation leads us over to the more general issue of the competences of the Government and the way and modes of the Parliament, in a parliamentarian system like the Swedish one, to supervise its activities.

§2. GOVERNMENTAL ACCOUNTABILITY IN RELATION TO PARLIAMENT

200. The basic rule in the Swedish constitution is, as mentioned above, that the government is accountable or responsible as a whole, or as a collective, as it is sometimes expressed, for its actions. As will be explained below, the individual responsibility and accountability is legally and formally limited (e.g., IG Chapter 7, Article 3 and Chapter 12, Article 2). Nevertheless, such accountability may be established, since the real scope of action of the individual minister is undoubtedly greater than those rules do indicate.[105] Individual ministers may of course also be held accountable for their political statements, comments, points of view etc., which may set the more specified rules on their accountability into motion. Thus, an individual accountability for ministers before the Parliament does exist, as follows clearly from the rules on the parliamentary vote of no-confidence.

201. Except for the strictly legal accountability mentioned above, the ministers are accountable only to the Parliament, whereas the civil servants are not, as may have been expected, legally accountable to the Parliament or the Government. Instead, they may be subject to the control conducted by the Ombudsman (cfr IG Chapter 13, Article 6), an original Swedish invention which is however legally speaking not extremely forceful. On the other hand, the civil servants have a full legal responsibility for their actions and may be prosecuted at any time for any irregularities conducted within their professional activities. In other words, they have no immunity at all. Also the general transparency within the public administration and the accessibility of documents is likely to contribute to the supervision of their activities, also from the media.

202. Legally speaking, the collective accountability means, as stated above, that the government as a whole is legally accountable and responsible for the Government's decisions, which are made at meetings where at least five ministers must be present (IG Chapter 7, Article 4). Obviously, illegalities or other irregularities are extremely rare in those kinds of decisions, but the only possibility to avoid such accountability is for the individual minister to have his or her dissenting opinion entered into the record from the Government meeting (IG 7:6). Should that actually happen – which is rare but not unique – the dissenting minister will not be held legally accountable for the decision. In the eyes of the public, he or she will probably also avoid political responsibility (but is on the other hand likely to see his or her influence within the government reduced).

105. This is also underlined in one of the leading constitutional comments, E. Holmberg/N. Stjernquist, Vår författning, 13th ed., Stockholm 2003, p. 132.

203. What could be further mentioned, however, is the unclear constitutional situation concerning the cooperation between the Social Democratic Government and two supporting parties, the Left and the Green Party, that took place from 1998 until 2006. The latter ones did then not form part of the Government and were thus formally not accountable for its decisions, but at the same time they did have advisors working in some Ministries and major political decisions, including budgetary ones, were made after negotiations between the Government and those parties. As mentioned above, this state of affairs was increasingly criticized for the very fact that it undermined political accountability in the traditional sense.

204. Furthermore, both decisions in relation to the budget and other political decisions are subject to *parliamentary control.* In fact, and as mentioned above, a special Chapter in the IG, Chapter 13, is devoted to this topic. As will be explained below, the possibility to declare a lack of confidence in a Minister is probably the most important part of the instruments at the Parliament's disposal in this respect (IG Chapter 13, Article 4). Apart from that, any member of the Riksdag may submit an interpellation or put a question to a minister on any matter concerning the minister's performance of his official duties (13:5). More detailed rules on those institutes are to be found in Chapter 6 of the Riksdag Act. A permission from the Speaker is necessary in order for the interpellation to be addressed to the Minister,[106] who is formally not obliged to answer. However, should an answer not be given within two weeks, an explanation for this behaviour is required.

205. The role of the Constitutional Committee, which is regulated in Chapter 13, Articles 1–2, is very important in this respect. The rules on the possibility for parliamentary committees to call or summon civil servants to questioning, in order to examine whether the government or individual ministers may have acted in-correctly in relation to public authorities or otherwise, are to be found in Chapter 4, Article 11 of the Riksdag Act.[107] Such meetings, where civil servants are asked to provide information, may be open to the public or not depending on the circumstances (Riksdag Act 4:13). It is however only a matter of providing information. Such persons are for instance never heard under oath. Civil servants working for authorities under the Government – i.e., the vast majority of the public bodies, as explained below – who doubt the wisdom of passing information to one of the different parliamentary committees, of which there are totally sixteen, may refer the request from the committee to the Government for a final decision on whether to occur before the committee or not (Riksdag Act 4:11).

106. Should the Speaker and the majority of the Riksdag not agree on whether the question may be put forward, the Constitutional Committee will have to decide the issue.

107. Those rules were enacted after the above-*mentioned* affair in 1988 concerning a private person, Mr Ebbe Carlsson, who had initiated his own investigations into the murder of the former PM and was supported in his actions by the Minister of Justice. The majority of the Constitutional Committee then found that open hearings could take place and that also civil servants should be called to those.

206. Debates in the chamber of the Swedish Parliament are normally open to the public, as mentioned above. Apart from debates and 'hearings' within the Committees, the Parliament may organize special hearings with experts. Such a hearing on the increased scope of separation of power in the traditional sense and the role of the courts was e.g., organized by the Constitutional Committee in March 2000 and, interestingly enough, the issue of accountability and control was discussed in the same way through a general discussion at a public hearing where no decisions were made in November 2005. Also the new Committee drafting constitutional amendments (*Grundlagsutredningen*), which is supposed to deliver proposals before the election in 2010, has organized two similar events in March and April 2005, as well as a number of seminars on constitutional issues.[108]

207. The other ways of exercising parliamentary control are through votes on lack of confidence and the control exercised by the Constitutional Committee. According to IG Chapter 13, Article 4, the Riksdag may at any time declare that a minister no longer enjoys its confidence, though such a declaration requires support of more than half the total membership of the Riksdag (i.e., 175 members). The motion calling for such a declaration must however be supported by at least one tenth of its members (i.e., 35). Such questions against individual members have been raised at various times, e.g., 1985 when the Foreign Minister Mr Bodström was accused of not supporting an official Swedish position against the Soviet Union concerning intruding submarines. However, such a motion has never been supported by the majority, but when the Minister of Justice Ms Leijon resigned in 1988, this was a direct consequence of the fact that the majority, consisting of right-wing parties and the Communist Party, had declared its will to vote against her.

208. The same procedure applies in relation to the PM, but as mentioned above, the difference is that if he or she should resign, the other ministers must also be discharged by the Speaker (IG 6:7). This could thus be described as a kind of 'collective dismissal'. However, it must be noted that, in a situation where the Parliament has declared its lack of confidence in a minister – the PM or another one – he or she does actually not have to resign if the Government may call for an extraordinary election within one week from the declaration. Such elections may never be called within three months from the date when a newly elected Riksdag is convened (IG Chapter 3, Article 11), but otherwise this possibility remains open for the Government in such a situation.[109]

108. The speeches of the two conferences in March and April 2005 are published in an unnumbered SOU 2005, called Behöver demokratin nya spelregler? The content of the thirty-seven speeches made there are commented by Nergelius in the Article Constitutionalism in Change – A Short Essay on (the Lack of) Contemporary Perspectives in the Swedish Debate, in Nergelius/O. Zetterquist (ed.), Law, State and Democracy in Multi-Level Governance, Stockholm 2006 (Stockholm Studies in Democratic Theory), pp. 46–57.

109. In June 1988, when Ms Leijon was forced to resign, this option was not interesting for the Government should she have chosen to face the vote of confidence, since an election was going to take place in September that year anyway. In fact, the government has never had to use this possibility.

209. As mentioned above, the PM may also in other situations dismiss Ministers at any time. In fact, the former PM Mr Persson did from March 1996, when he took office, until September 2006 dispose over a total of fifty-one Ministers, although only some twenty are sitting in the Government simultaneously. This also reflects the increasingly strong position of the PM, which is now starting to be criticized in the doctrine and even sometimes described as 'presidential' in its nature.

210. It must also be mentioned that every year, the Constitutional Committee exercises an examination of the ministers' individual performance of their official duties, as well as the handling of Government business in general. The Committee writes an annual report to the Parliament on its observations, which is quite often a matter of political controversy. However, the party representation in the various parliamentary committees, including this one, corresponds to the situation in the Parliament as a whole, which makes open criticism against the Government somewhat less likely and unusual. The President of the Constitutional Committee does however always represent the opposition. And should the majority of the Committee reach the conclusion that criticism against a minister is required, it will state so in its report (a so-called '*prickning*', which may be politically sensitive but lacks formal legal significance). An incident in 2014 illustrated that ministers and in particular former ministers do not have any legal obligation to occur before the committee, although a failure to show up there may of course harm their reputation.

211. In order for the Committee to fulfil its duties, it is entitled to have access to the records of decisions taken in Government matters and all the documents pertaining to such matters that it finds necessary in order to conduct the investigation properly (Chapter 13, Article 1, section 1). It may also act upon the observations of other committees.[110]

212. In relation not least to EU matters and, albeit indirectly, the resignation of the Commission in March 1999, also the birth of the new National Audit Office, which is since 2002 regulated in IG Chapter 12, Article 7, is of great interest. This new public authority resides under the Parliament and has replaced both the old National Audit Office, which worked under the Government, and the so-called Parliamentary Accountants, who were politicians and acting MP's![111] It may be of a certain interest to know that this new office was in a way born out of a huge and highly public conflict in 1999 between the former Managing Director of the old National Audit Office (*Riksrevisionsverket*) Ms Inga-Britt Ahlenius, and the former Minister of Finance Mr Ringholm. Ms Ahlenius, who was also a member of the Group of Experts whose report in March 1999 led the EU Commission to resign (and who does now hold a very high position as a kind of 'super-accountant' within the UN), advocated strongly in favour of creating this new, independent auditing office and did thus, finally, 'win' this battle with the Government.

110. Those rules on the Constitutional Committee are to be found in Ch. 12, Arts 1–2 IG, as mentioned above.

111. The new agency is called, in Swedish, *Riksrevisionen*. It has thus replaced both the former bodies Riksrevisionsverket and Riksdagens revisorer.

213. This new office is under the direction of three Auditors General, who are elected by the Riksdag and decide independently what activities that shall be audited. When conclusions from the audit are drawn, the Board of the office puts forward to the Riksdag the proposals and reports which result, as well as the official audit statements.

214. To summarize, vote on lack of confidence for a certain minister and the annual reports of the Constitutional Committee are the two main instruments for the Swedish Parliament to exercise its control over the Government. In the future, the reports of the National Audit Office may also come to be very important, though that remains to be seen. Further reform proposals are from time to time suggested in the debate. Thus, the topic is a 'living' one within the doctrine.[112] However, it should be noted that *Grundlagsutredningen*, the newly appointed committee dealing with constitutional reform, has not been instructed to look into this particular issue.[113]

215. It should also be noted that the system of political accountability for the government was vividly discussed in the first week of December 2005, as a result of the report from the special Commission on the responsibility for mishandling of the consequences of the *Tsunami* in south-east Asia on 26 December 2004, in which some 600 Swedish citizens died.[114] The report was clear in placing the main responsibility for things that had not functioned during and after the catastrophe on the government and the Prime Minister in particular. The main criticism was that a national alert system in times of catastrophes and urgent crisis had never been installed. Thus, the public authorities had no real instructions and simply did not know exactly how to act in this totally unexpected and unforeseen situation.

216. In the aftermath of the report, it was much discussed whether the opposition parties should have called for a vote on lack of confidence against the Prime Minister, in line with IG Chapter 13, Article 4, and thus against the whole government. Finally, on 6 December 2005, they decided not to do so but to wait instead for the inquiry that the Constitutional Committee was going to start. But in view of the very sharp criticism already launched in the report, together with the previous situations e.g., in 1980, 1985 or 1996, when such votes have been called for what seems to be less severe errors, this decision does not seem to be entirely logical. It shall thus be viewed in light of the fact that a new Parliamentary election was going to take place in September 2006, which meant that the opposition had an obvious political interest in keeping the issue 'alive' as much as possible until then, rather

112. See, among others, J. Höök/O. Lundin, Kontroll och ansvarsutkrävande i svensk offentlig förvaltning, Nordiskt Administrativt Tidsskrift 2001, pp. 117–128 and J. Ekroth, Några reflektioner angående Konstitutionsutskottets granskning av regeringen, in N. Berggren/N. Karlson/J. Nergelius (ed.), Makt utan motvikt – Om demokrati och konstitutionalism, Stockholm 1999, pp. 189–235. Among political scientists, see among others L. Lewin, Bråka inte! – Om vår tids demokratisyn, Stockholm 1999.

113. Its instructions are to be found in Kommittédirektiv 2004:96.

114. The full title of the report is Sverige och tsunamin – granskning och förslag, SOU 2005:104.

than seeing it formally settled by such a vote almost a year in advance. In particular, this was the case since it seemed clear that the Government's supporting parties, i.e., the Left and the Green Party, would not have voted against the Prime Minister should such a vote have taken place. Still, from a legal and constitutional point of view, the decision not to ask for such a vote here was hardly justified.

217. Instead, the Constitutional Committee of the Parliament came to examine the behaviour of the Government during and after the tsunami quite thoroughly, as a part of its regular supervision of the Government. In fact, the opposition parties placed some lawyers and other MP's who are legal experts within the Committee for those particular hearings, which somehow seemed to be intended to underline their legal and not exclusively political nature. The findings of the Committee are to be found in the report KU 2005/06:8,[115] presented in March 2006, in which sharp formal criticism was raised against a number of ministers, including the Prime Minister and the Foreign Minister. Thus, a 'prickning' did in fact occur here. However, the Foreign Minister, Ms Freivalds, choose to resign in March 2006 before the report was published, allegedly for mishandling of issues related to the Danish so-called *Muhammed crisis* but in reality acting as a scapegoat for the whole government after the tsunami event. After that, the opposition parties decided not to raise a vote of confidence against the PM or any other minister.

218. Without criticizing the existing Swedish rules in this field as such, which would be futile when they have actually existed for quite a long time and will obviously not be subject to revision for yet quite long – partly because they are considered to be a part of the existing constitutional tradition – a few distinctive features, that are in fact slightly problematic, may after all be identified.

219. One such feature is the important but quite puzzling role of the Constitutional Committee, KU. As mentioned above, the parliamentary examination of how the government has conducted its activities in the past year is done mainly through the works of this body (Chapter 13, Article 2 IG). As far as the political examination is concerned, the main problem here seems to be that the party representation within the committee is the same as for the parliament as a whole, a fact which reduces the possibility of the opposition to criticize the government for mismanagement of certain issues. But even more puzzling, perhaps, is the tendency clearly shown through the hearings on the Tsunami aftermath, namely that the work of the Constitutional Committee also tends to be of a legal character. This is a kind of examination, then, the legal basis of which is unclear and does not follow clearly from the IG (where the rules in Chapter 13, Articles 1–2 do actually not distinguish between different kinds of control in this way). However, from the accountability point of view, it seems clear that the supervision exercised by the Constitutional Committee must above all be a political one (which does not exclude that clear violations of law, like the one made by Ms Leijon in 1988, may be subject to political

115. The full official title of which is Granskning av regeringens krisberedskap och krishantering i samband med flodvågskatastrofen 2004, vols. 1–3, KU 2005/06:8.

criticism, since a minister who violates the law is not likely to be handling the job very well and may of course also make a political error, at the same time).

220. Another clear feature is of course the very strong emphasis on parliamentarianism and popular sovereignty within the whole Swedish constitutional system. From the accountability point of view, perhaps the absence of any control as such of the activities of the Parliament, the legislative branch, is the clearest example of this. 'Parliamentary control' in the sense of Chapter 13 IG does obviously only refer to the control exercised by the Parliament over the other branches of Government. Still, the somewhat strengthened role of the courts mentioned below must also be observed.

221. From a practical point of view, apart from the absence of a strong system of judicial review and the relatively weak general position of the courts, the judicial branch, this is perhaps most visible through the model of so-called 'negative parliamentarianism' that is used when a new PM and thus a new government is being appointed. The fact that this can – and does in fact regularly – take place with the support of only a minority of the MP's does obviously lead to a tradition of weak governments. At the same time, another interesting feature or pattern, that Sweden seems to share with UK, is that a strong formal emphasis on parliamentarianism does actually lead to a situation where the government is the stronger actor that regularly takes initiatives and has the ability to force the Parliament to obey its wishes. It seems clear that a strong parliamentarianism does not automatically lead to efficient modes of political accountability. On the contrary, a situation where the government is supported by a majority of the Parliament without actually comprising or representing parties that possess such a majority may actually be described as the worst possible as far as political accountability is concerned.

§3. Governmental Accountability in Relation to Public Authorities

222. The basic features of the Swedish Constitution, as outlined above, also mean that ministers as individuals or the government as a whole is accountable mainly for policy-making, but not for the execution or implementation of its own decisions. This is a fact that has to do with the traditionally high level of autonomy of the Swedish public administration and its bodies (*myndigheter*).[116]

223. According to IG Chapter 12, Article 2, no public authority, including the Parliament and the Government, may determine how an administrative authority shall decide in a particular case relating to the exercise of public authority vis-à-vis

116. For various reasons, the concept of 'agencies' does not seem to fit well with the Swedish system and terminology as far as the public administration is concerned, since the Swedish system knows only the concept of Public Authority ('myndighet' or 'förvaltningsmyndighet'). Such administrative authority may be delegated to companies, associations, foundations etc. (IG Ch. 11, Art. 6, s. 3), but the scope of such delegation is limited. A study from 1989 that deals with administration outside the traditional realm of public authorities is L. Marcusson, Offentlig förvaltning utanför myndighetsområdet (Iustus, Uppsala).

a private subject or a local authority, or relating to the application of law. In the constitutional doctrine and in the settled practice of the political bodies, this has for a long time been interpreted to mean that the ministers may not interfere in the concrete, specific activities of the administrative bodies.[117] An interesting case in order to illustrate this may be the events following the assassination of Prime Minister Olof Palme in 1986, which may now be analysed a little bit closer. In 1988, it was revealed that the Minister of Justice Ms Anna-Greta Leijon had written a letter of recommendation to a private friend, Mr Ebbe Carlsson, in order to help him conduct certain private investigations related to the murder, on the cause of which he had certain theories. While cooperating with a few policemen who shared his views, his actions and investigations, which included some illegal acts, were not sanctioned by the responsible police authorities or the officers in charge of the official murder investigation. Thus, the way in which the Minister of Justice had supported his private activities, without informing the police authorities, provoked harsh protests from the police and was seen as an illegal and unconstitutional involvement in police affairs from the Minister, who later had to resign as explained above.

224. Thus, ministers do normally not have the power to interfere in the work of public authorities or give detailed instructions to civil servants, though general political guidelines are of course allowed. At the same time, however, ministers are normally not accountable or responsible for the actions of public authorities. Once again, a discussion on the role of the Minister of Justice may illustrate the situation. In the summer of 2004, a number of heavily guarded prisoners escaped from different Swedish prisons. The right-wing opposition then asked for the resignation of the Minister of Justice, but since he could not be held accountable or responsible for the errors or mistakes made by responsible civil servants in the relevant public bodies, those demands had no legal or constitutional base. Only if the minister has known for some time about problems in specific bodies without reacting or doing anything about them (something that was actually discussed in relation to those events) may the minister be held legally or politically accountable.[118]

225. In this way, there may thus be said to exist a clear relation between the scope of accountability and responsibility of the ministers, which is very limited as far as the actions and decisions of the public authorities for which they are politically responsible is concerned, and their legal powers, which are also limited in relation to those authorities. It should be noted that a Parliamentary Committee appointed in 2003, the so-called *Ansvarskommittén*, was told to look into the effects of this traditional autonomy and independence of the public authorities. From the government, it was then argued that this independence does not work well in relation to the EU, e.g., whenever EU ministerial or committee meetings are held.

117. It may be noted that IG 12:2 does not apply to the Government itself, since that is not an *administrative* authority ('föruältningsmyndighet').
118. Yet another Minister of Justice, Mr Wickbom, was forced to resign when a convicted spy (Mr Stig Bergling) managed to escape in 1987, but this was contrary to how the system normally works and actually mainly reflected his weak position within the Government. Due to discussion on his general competence and ability, the PM after the escape decided to replace him with Ms Leijon, who was then forced to resign less than a year later for quite different reasons, as mentioned above.

However, it looks unlikely that this committee did not propose any changes in this area.[119]

226. It should also be added here that almost all public authorities work under the Government, unless the Constitution or a law expressly state that they work under the Parliament (IG Chapter 12, Article 1). Ministers are also responsible and accountable for the actions of their political advisors. The work of those advisors does often form a most important part of the political decision-making of the minister, of which however he or she must be fully accountable. Thus, the role of the advisors is not regulated as such by the constitution or by other laws.

227. This leads us over to the structure of two peculiar Chapters in the IG, which are now less unlogical seen from an international perspective but which still reflect the mixed character of the Swedish constitution, somewhere between a total emphasis on popular sovereignty and a wish to protect the independence of the courts and other public authorities without giving them any real powers, namely its Chapters 11–12.

228. Here, a big change took place in 2010, when the courts were finally given a chapter of their own (Chapter 11). Chapter 11 deals, according to its title, with 'Administration of justice'. In other words, this means that the courts and the other public authorities are no longer placed together, in the same Chapter, but each have a chapter of its own. In a way, this current order seems to reflect the traditionally strong position of the public authorities and the similarly weak position of the courts within the Swedish constitutional system – a tradition that may now indeed be questioned.

229. As mentioned above, most of the public authorities reside under the Government, in accordance with Chapter 12, Article 1, section 1 IG, unless they reside under the Parliament according to the IG. The latter is the case e.g., concerning the Ombudsman (*Justitieombudsmannen, JO*, who is officially *Riksdagens ombudsman*, Chapter 13, Article 6), the National Audit Office, Chapter 13, Article 7 and the National Bank (Chapter 9, Article 13). Since this structure is in fact very clear, one might wonder why the Chancellor of Justice (*Justitiekanslern, JK*),[120]) is in fact mentioned specifically in Chapter 12, Article 1 IG, but regardless of the reason for that, we can see that the Swedish administrative organization clearly contains many distinctive features.

---

119. Its main, final report SOU 2007:10, Hållbar samhällsorganisation med utvecklingskraft, is in fact entirely devoted to the future regional organization of Sweden, as will be discussed below in Part III.

120. This is in fact the only place in the IG where the Chancellor of Justice, who is traditionally seen as the attorney or even 'ombudsman' of the State or rather the government is mentioned. He does however have a number of important but rather various and different tasks, like supervising the lawyers, representing the state in prosecutions falling under FPA or FSA and also to negotiate on behalf of the state in tort issues.

230. One such feature is the hierarchical structure with several authorities working in different sectors, where the main, central authority, residing under the ministry, may have various authorities, including local ones, working under itself.[121] It must also be observed that a minister, according to this structure and the rules on accountability mentioned above, regardless of whether he is head of a ministry or not (cfr IG Chapter 7, Articles 1 and 5), will never be in a position to be 'head' or 'boss' of any public agency or authority, in the sense that he should have any influence on its daily business.

231. Thus, the administration is divided into a government office (IG Chapter 7, Article 1) and independent, centrally located public authorities, a historic heritage that can be traced back to circa 1632, after the death of king Gustav II Adolf, when his chancellor Axel Oxenstierna, pending the reign of the young princess Kristina, re-organized and centralized the Swedish administration and probably turned it into the most modern in the world. It is different from the one reigning in most parliamentarian systems like for instance in the United Kingdom. In constitutional terms, it means that the government may give guidelines to the authorities in terms of general policies – which the authorities have to obey – but not in terms of how they are to decide in individual cases. This independence is specifically regulated in Chapter 12, Article 2 IG, which states that no public authority, including the Parliament and the decision-making bodies of local authorities, may determine how an administrative authority shall decide in a particular case relating to the exercise of public authority vis-à-vis a private subject[122] or a local authority, or relating to the application of law.[123] In their settlement of specific cases, the public authorities, like the courts, are of course bound to observe and respect the so-called objectivity principle in IG Chapter 1, Article 9.

232. Decisions made by the Governments in administrative matters may be subject to re-opening (*resning*) under certain circumstances, IG Chapter 11, Article 13, which would then take place at the Supreme Administrative Court. On the other hand, the Government may according to Chapter 12, Article 9 exercise clemency (*nåd*) or even order, on exceptional ground, that no further action shall be taken to investigate or prosecute a criminal act (*abolition*) and thus interfere with the work of prosecutors or judicial bodies. However, none of those possibilities are practically very important.

233. A number of parliamentary committees have in recent years studied this issue and also proposed reforms, in order to make it easier for the government to

121. An excellent study of this structure and its legal implications is made by J. Höök/O. Lundin, Kontroll och ansvarsutkrävande i svensk offentlig förvaltning, Nordiskt Administrativt Tidskrift 2001, pp. 117–130. It may be added that rules on the internal organization of a public authority are to be found in the so-called *Verksförordningen* from 1995.
122. This concept corresponds to what is in Swedish called *myndighetsutövning mot enskild*, a term that may actually be hard to define and limit but which covers and includes all kind of exercise of public power, by the authorities against individuals.
123. Also the above-mentioned prohibition against legislation for specific cases in IG Ch. 11, Art. 4 shall of course be mentioned in this respect.

instruct the public authorities and thereby strengthen the power of the Government. Still, the independence of the public authorities may have a big value, which may partly explain the low degree of corruption in Sweden although one political party has been so dominant for seventy-five years. Finally, the independence of the public authorities (or 'agencies') and the prohibition against any governmental interference in their handling of specific cases may even be described as a positive element of the Swedish constitution, notably from the accountability perspective since any violation of this principle (which is constitutionally protected by IG Chapter 11, Article 3 (courts) and Chapter 12, Article 2 (public agencies)) is easily discernible, as shown once again through the example of Ms Leijon in 1988.

234. The system also seems to work remarkably well in relation to the constitutional point of departure, IG Chapter 1, Article 6 which states that 'The Government governs the Realm. It is accountable to the Riksdag'. That is actually how the system is working, though many observers have in recent years observed the increasing strength of the Government – and not least the PM – in relation to the Parliament.

Chapter 5. The Judiciary and the Independence of the Courts

§1. Judicial Organization

235. Concerning the position of the courts, it shall first be observed that the rule in IG Chapter 11, Article 4 according to which no judicial or administrative function may normally be performed by the Parliament entails a strong protection also for judicial independence, since it means that the Parliament may never try to reverse an individual judgment through legislation. Apart from that, a very important rule is to be found in Chapter 11, Article 3, which states that no public authority, including the Riksdag, may determine how a court of law shall adjudicate an individual case or otherwise apply a rule of law in a particular case. Although no traditional separation of power is expected to occur in Sweden, at least not in the traditional sense and in any way less than it did in the old Constitution of 1809 (as follows from Chapter 1, Article 1 IG), this provision has actually strengthened the position of the courts compared to the old constitution, which is worth noticing.

236. Also a few other rules are important in this respect. According to Chapter 2, Article 11 IG, no court of law shall be established on account of an act already committed, or for a particular dispute or otherwise for a particular case.[124] Furthermore, if a public authority other than a court has deprived a citizen of his liberty on account of a criminal act or because he is suspected of having committed such an act, he shall be entitled to have the matter examined before a court without undue delay under Chapter 2, Article 9.[125] Finally, it shall be observed that according to Chapter 11, Article 5, a legal dispute between private subjects may not be settled by any other authority than a court of law except by virtue of law (which may for instance allow private arbitration bodies). Apart from that rule, however, there are no constitutional provisions requiring that a certain type of cases should always be tried by courts, a fact that probably contributed to the many condemning judgments against Sweden from the Strasbourg court in the 1990s.[126] And of the different courts that exist in Sweden, only the Supreme Court (*Högsta Domstolen*) and the Supreme Administrative Court (*Regeringsrätten*) are in fact mentioned in the IG (in Chapter 11, Article 1, which also mentions that the right to have a case tried in these two instances may be restricted in law).[127] Other courts must be established by virtue of law.

124. It is worth noting that the same restriction does not apply in relation to public authorities, which makes it easier to establish such temporary bodies for the examination of specific affairs or scandals, like e.g., the handling of the Tsunami.
125. There is one exception from this rule, namely if the question relates to the transfer to Sweden of responsibility for executing a penal sanction involving deprivation of liberty which has been imposed in another state.
126. Gradually, those flaws in the Swedish judicial system have been remedied by changes in the Administrative Law and the enactment of the so-called Rättsprövningslagen (from 1988 but changed in 2006), the aim of which simply is to make more administrative decisions than before susceptible to review by a court of law. Those reforms are important and maybe even by now, i.e., since 2006, sufficient in order to avoid violations of Art. 6 ECHR.
127. Something that has in fact been the case for a long time, since those courts only try cases with a principled interest, having granted a so-called right for appeal or petition (*prövningstillstånd*).

237. From this, we learn at least two things. First, it is clear that the Swedish court system consists of general and administrative courts, working side by side and both with three instances.[128] While the general courts, where the proceedings are mainly oral, deal with criminal and civil cases, the administrative courts, whose procedures are mainly written, mostly deal with appeals against decisions in various matters made by the public authorities. Apart from that, also some important special courts exist, like the Labour Court (*Arbetsdomstolen*) and the Market Court (*Marknadsdomstolen*). The existence of such courts, where representatives of interest groups may even be in a majority, has sometimes been put in question, but the Labour Court was in fact 'approved' by the European Court of Human Rights in October 2004 as a proper court in the sense of the Convention.[129] Still, the absence in the Swedish constitution on detailed rules about which cases and disputes that need to be examined by courts may partly, together with a deep historic tradition of an independent administration, explain the big number of cases where Swedish citizens have complained before the Strasbourg court on alleged violations of Article 6 ECHR. A number of reforms concerning in particular the administrative courts have however been enacted in recent years and as mentioned above, the sitting or working Constitutional Reform Committee is also considering devoting a special Chapter in the IG to the Courts, instead of letting them 'share' Chapter 11 with the other public authorities.

§2. Legal Status of the Judges

238. Judges in the two Supreme Courts must hold an appointment as a permanent salaried justice of the court where he works, while the requirement for other courts simply is that they shall at least have one permanent, salaried judge[130] (although they do of course normally have more than one).

239. Appointments to posts at courts of law or administrative authorities coming under the Government are made by the Government (Chapter 11, Article 6, section 1 IG). Concerning the removal of judges, legal proceedings on account of a criminal act committed by a member of the Supreme Court or the Supreme Administrative Court in the exercise of his official duties shall according to Chapter 11, Article 8 IG be instituted in the Supreme Court by the Parliamentary Ombudsman or the Chancellor of Justice. The Supreme Court likewise examines, under similar conditions, whether a member of one of the two courts shall be removed from office or suspended from duty, or obliged to undergo examination by a medical practitioner. Thus, judges of the Supreme Court may in this way be required to pass

128. The general courts are divided into Tingsrätt-Hovrätt-Högsta Domstolen, while the three administrative court instances are called Länsrätt-Kammarrätt-Regeringsrätten.
129. Case *Kellermann*, 41579/98, Judgment 26 Oct. 2004. In a previous case in 1989 (Langborger, 22 Jun. 1989, Series A, No. 155), the former, less-known but very similar Housing Court (Bostadsdomstolen) was however not seen to meet the requirements of Art. 6 ECHR as an independent court. After that, it simply ceased to exist.
130. Ch. 11, Art. 1, s. 3 IG.

judgment on one of their colleagues, which is definitely not an ideal situation.[131] For other judges, a special rule in Chapter 11, Article 7 applies, according to which a person who has been appointed as a permanent salaried judge may be removed from office only if he has shown himself through a criminal act or through gross or repeated neglect of his official duties to be manifestly unfit to hold the office or if he has reached the relevant retirement age or is otherwise obliged by law to retire on pension.

240. Should a permanent salaried judge have been removed from office by means of a decision of a public authority other than a court of law, or suspended from duty or ordered to undergo examination by a medical practitioner, it shall be possible for him to call for the decision to be examined by a court (see Chapter 11, Article 9). This protection of the services of judges has often been criticized as being too weak, not least since the court in question would in most cases be the Labour Court, basically composed by a majority of laymen judges representing the labour organizations. It may even be questioned if this order is compatible with Article 6 of the European Convention of Human Rights with its guarantee for a *fair trial*.[132] From that same point of view, also the rule in Chapter 11, Article 2 according to which provisions concerning the functions of the courts relevant to the administration of justice, the principal feature of their organization and court procedure are laid down in law may be criticized, since it seems to give the Government or the relevant public authority (the so-called *Domstolsverket*), or even the President of a court, rather wide competences to distribute cases between different judges and interfere in other sensitive issues. From the last few years, it may be noted that this Court Authority has decided to pay (permanent) salaries to judges on an individual basis, based on their skills, a practice that seems to be highly doubtful to say the least.

241. Concerning the appointment of judges as well as other public officials, attention shall according to Chapter 11, Article 6, section 2 IG only be directed to objective factors such as merit and competence. Thus, foreigners would at least formally have the same possibilities as Swedes to apply for those posts, where merit represents the number of years of professional experience within a given field and competence equalizes the individual skills. Still, merit and competence are only some of the requirements needed ('such as'), which makes the criteria and the appointment procedure slightly more blurred. In recent years, the issue of equality between men and women has gained much attention, but it is after all not likely that a less qualified woman could get a post for which a more qualified man has also applied.[133]

131. The issue is far from theoretical, as shown in 2005 when it was revealed that a judge at the Supreme Court, Mr Thorsson, had violated the law by purchasing sexual services from a male prostitute. However, the Chancellor of Justice in a contested decision did not initiate any proceedings against the judge in question.
132. Cfr Nergelius, *supra*, p. 246.
133. This follows in part from the case *Abrahamsson et al. v. Fogelqvist*, concerning academic chairs reserved for women, which was settled by ECJ in 2000 (C-407/98, ECR 2000 I, p. 5539).

Part III. The State and Its Subdivisions

§1. Distribution of Powers between the State and the Municipalities

242. The traditionally very centralized Swedish state has during the last ten years, in particular after joining the EU in 1995, been severely affected of what we may here call a vertical separation of powers, upwards in relation to the EU, as described above in Part II, Chapter 3, and downwards in relation to a gradually increasing development towards stronger regionalization, which is accompanied also by the traditional strong autonomy of the municipalities.

243. Concerning the latter question, the point of departure is that Swedish democracy, according to IG Chapter 1, Article 1, section 2 is based and realized, among other values, upon local self-government. Somewhat more detailed rules are to be found in Chapter 1, Article 7, which states that Sweden has municipalities and county councils *(landsting)*. This rule also used to state that the decision-making power in these local authorities is exercised by elected assemblies and that the local authorities may levy taxes in order to perform their tasks,[134] but this rule is now moved to a new Chapter 14 that deals exclusively with the municipalities (without really increasing their autonomy, unfortunately). Chapter 1, Article 8 also reveals that central and local government administrative authorities exist for 'the public administration', which may thus be either national or local.[135]

244. Still, all those rules are rather general and vague. Some more precise rules may be found on the topic, like Chapter 8, Article 2, section 1 point 3 IG, according to which the principles governing changes in the division of the Realm into local government districts, as well as the principles governing the organization and working procedures of the local authorities and their competences are laid down in law,[136] but a further analysis of the legal conditions for local and the recently so

134. Here, once again, it may be noted that the Government may never adopt provisions which relate to local taxation, according to IG Ch. 8, Art. 7, s. 2, 2nd sentence. On the other hand, municipalities or the Government may under certain conditions make decision concerning burdensome charges that should otherwise be made by the Parliament, as follows from Ch. 8, Art. 9 IG.

135. Something that does in fact also follow from IG Ch. 12, Art. 4, s. 2, which specifically states that administrative functions may be entrusted to a local authority.

136. Also a few other provisions may be noted here. Thus, whenever the Parliament has authorized the Government to adopt provisions in a particular matter under Ch. 8 IG, it may also according to its Art. 10 authorize the Government to delegate the power to adopt regulations in the matter to an

much discussed regional autonomy in Sweden definitely seems to be necessary to conduct here.

245. Sweden is, as mentioned above, a unitary, highly centralized nation-state, where federalism has never been a realistic alternative and regionalization is a very recent phenomenon, with two attempts of regional autonomy being carried out since 1998 and continuing until at least 2010 (in Skåne, the southern part of Sweden, and Västra Götaland, centred around Gothenburg in the west part of the country).[137] Alongside with this centralized tradition, a high degree of local autonomy has existed since 1862, when an important reform in that respect took place.[138] The extent of the local and to be more precise municipal autonomy is however a highly contested issue. It must be noted that regardless of which rules that do really apply here, the competences may obviously be shifted between the state and the municipalities; thus, the organization of the police force used to be local, but became national in the 1960s. And conversely, the school system turned into a local, or rather municipal affair in the early 1990s. It is obvious that the municipal autonomy is not strong enough to be a real obstacle against major reforms of this kind.[139]

246. In the constitutional doctrine, the opinions have been very divided, ranging from old-fashioned state-oriented professors who truly believe that the state (Parliament, Government) may limit the municipal autonomy as it wishes (in particular Sterzel), to younger constitutionalists like myself who believe that the above-*mentioned* constitutional provisions must after all mean something and that they do thus offer a minimum of constitutional protection for the municipal autonomy. When the IG was enacted in the 1970s the former opinion undoubtedly prevailed,[140] but on this like on many other issues the opinion(s) have since then been slightly modified. That new, opposite opinion has above all been advanced by the Law Council when examining a number of law proposals in the late 1990s and in the beginning of the twenty-first century, concerning transfer of money through a system for re-distribution of taxes between rich and poor municipalities (*inomkommunal skatteutjämning*), a prohibition for municipalities to sell their housing companies, for county councils to let certain hospitals be organized privately or an obligation for municipalities to organize agencies for housing transfer. In all those cases, when the Law Council has recommended that the laws in question should not be enacted, the Parliament has approved them anyway.

---

administrative or local authority (so-called sub-delegation). Finally, it should once again be noted that administrative functions may be entrusted to local authorities according to Ch. 12, Art. 4, s. 2 IG.

137. A sign of the new times and the new climate in the debate, where it is now possible to seriously discuss also federalism, is the anthology *Federalism på svenska* (Federalism in Swedish), ed. by N. Karlson/J. Nergelius, Stockholm 2007 (Ratio).

138. Cfr Nergelius, *supra*, p. 287 s.

139. In both cases it may be noted that many critics want to turn the system back the other way around once again, which is at least not constitutionally impossible.

140. This is perhaps most clearly expressed in a governmental bill (proposition) from 1973, which contains much of the principled reasoning that is included in the IG (prop. 1973:90, here on p. 190).

247. From a legal point of view, maybe the first question to ask here is whether the provisions of IG mentioned above are really legally binding or not. Chapter 1, Article 1 IG is a non-binding principled provision, like many other parts of Chapter 1 (e.g., Chapter 1, Article 2). Chapter 8, Article 2 is on the other hand clearly binding, but does in fact not mean anything else than that the Parliament may decide certain things concerning municipal activities through law. The former Chapter 1, Article 7, section 2 (now Chapter 14, Article 4) was more open to different interpretations, but anyway seemed to mean that local authorities may only levy taxes from their inhabitants for the fulfilment of various tasks and municipalities within that municipality, an interpretation that is supported by the Municipal Law (*Kommunallagen*) Chapter 2, Article 1 and that would seem to make transfers of money from certain municipalities to others, like the ones decided upon by the Parliament from 1995 and onwards, in order to transfer money to poorer parts of the country, illegal and unconstitutional.[141] However, the new Chapter 14, Article 5 makes clear that they are now to be considered legal. The question has never really been tried or examined by the Swedish courts, since both the Supreme Court and the Supreme Administrative Court decided in cases 1998 and 2000, concerning the same issue, that the complaining municipalities were not allowed to have their cases heard before those courts![142] From many points of view, it is regrettable that the courts refused to deal with the case, in a manner that would, for the total effect considered, even amount to a kind of *déni de justice*.[143]

248. In fact, it would also be almost impossible for the municipalities to fulfil the main part of the tasks that they are actually ordered by law to perform and be responsible for (cfr IG Chapter 8, Article 2, section 1 point 3) if they were not free to decide upon how to tax their inhabitants and how to use the taxes thus raised. If they were not able to control and plan their economy themselves, they would not be autonomous in the way that IG says that they are and must be, in order for the Swedish democracy to be fully realized. Thus, a certain kind of minimum constitutional protection for their rights simply must be said to exist. But as mentioned above, in particular during the late 1990s but also now, the limits of this autonomy has been a hotly contested issue, which may in purely political terms be explained by the fact that when the Social Democratic Party stayed in power for so long at the national level, the possibility to conduct another kind of policy at the local level in the municipalities where it stayed in majority became ever more interesting for the right-wing opposition – a development and tendency that the Government then became increasingly interested in stopping, in line with a certain political logic.[144] Such a reaction may, apart from in purely political terms, also be justified with the aim of assuring that citizens are treated equally in all parts of the country.[145] In purely political terms, this perspective is the one that has won in the discussions

141. See *more* in detail Nergelius, *supra*, p. 289 ss with further references.
142. See NJA 1998, p. 656 (II) and RÅ 2000 ref. 19.
143. For legal reasons, the municipalities, formally being components of the State, were also unable to bring their cases to the Strasbourg court.
144. Cfr Nergelius, *supra*, in particular p. 295 s.
145. This issue is particularly dealt with and analysed in the anthology edited by Karlson and Nergelius, mentioned above.

leading to the big constitutional compromise that will now become a reality and enter into force in 2010.

249. Both the two changes considered urgent in the first edition of this volume, then, namely more precise rules in the Constitution guaranteeing the protection of the autonomy of the municipalities and a system where elections to the municipalities would take place on some other time than the national elections, have now partly been realized – although the autonomy as such of the municipalities, in legal terms, has not grown.

§2. The Regional Issue

250. As mentioned above, in recent years a vivid debate has been starting in Sweden concerning future regionalization, which is noteworthy and slightly surprising as such in this old nation-state. One reason for this is the weakness of the old county councils (*landsting*), which are not to be reckoned with as serious political actors in an era where regions in many other European states are becoming ever more important and cooperation across traditional national frontiers is also a clear tendency, as shown from examples both in southern, western and northern Sweden.

251. Against this general background, two important things that have happened in recent years and have thus contributed to making the issue more important than before, are the attempts of introducing regional autonomy in the southern part of the country (Skåne) and in a western area around Gothenburg (Västra Götaland), which are now permanent, as well as the end report in February 2007 of the national committee examining the future division of the country and future organization of welfare and social service[146] (the so-called Ansvarskommittén).[147] This report suggests a division of Sweden into either six or nine regions (or seven or eight, possibly), the organization of which has been much contested, due in particular to the many different regional interests that are vested into such a big reform. Those regions would then be responsible for the organization not only of hospitals and medical care, but also for transportation and environmental issues. What then happened, however, is that the regions of Västra Götaland and Skåne have been given almost a kind of permanent license to continue their activities, while no decisions have yet been made concerning other parts of the country. Also Gotland in the Baltic Sea and Halland in the south-west are now called regions, as well as five other territories as of 1 January 2015, but in these cases it is mainly a matter of changing name from district or "län" to "region"; neither their frontiers or territories, nor their competences are really affected by this change.

146. Concerning welfare issues, that was dealt with in a previous report from 2003 (SOU 2003:123, Utvecklingskraft för hållbar välfärd).

147. The official title of which is SOU 2007:10, Hållbar samhällsorganisation med utvecklingskraft.

252. It should however be noted that there is still no political consensus on those issues. In the former, right-wing government, the suggestions made by Ansvarskommittén are not supported by the biggest, conservative party, which is currently bigger than the three other governmental parties together. Thus, the issue has been left for future decision-making. The position of the Social Democratic party and the left-wing opposition, on the other hand, has moved in a more region-friendly direction in the last few years.

253. The arguments raised in the debate, in favour of increased regionalization, in particular have to do with how and to which – great – extent that the regions do in fact today affect the lives of individuals, who increasingly tend to commute, work and live in certain regions rather than in municipalities, as well as the tendency of new regions to identify and market themselves as regions, for instance by opening offices in Brussels. That is true both for regions who want to be active internationally, like Skåne, and regions who in particular want to be heard within the country, like the so-called *Mälardal* area around Stockholm. Apart from that, strengthened regional identities among individuals, wishes for increased democracy and new means to organize, provide and distribute welfare services are other well-known arguments from the debate in the last few years. It remains to be seen which impact they will have on the final reform proposals in this area. What seems certain, anyway, is that the issue is here to stay and that some reform, including both municipalities and regions, will eventually take place some time after 2010.

Part IV. Human Rights and Judicial Review

Chapter 1. Human Rights in Sweden

§1. General Remarks

254. The applicable and binding rules on human rights in Sweden are to be found in Chapter 2 IG, in the Freedom of Press Act of 1949 and the Freedom of Speech Act from 1991, as far as freedom of speech in books and the media is concerned, and finally the European Convention of Human Rights, which applies as domestic Swedish law since 1995. Since this is a book on Swedish constitutional law, there is in fact no need to go through the well-known European Convention, but the other three constitutional acts all need to be closer presented and analysed.

255. Still, a few words could be said concerning the background of the incorporation of the European Convention of Human Rights into Swedish law. As mentioned above, Sweden is a typical example of what is normally called a *dualist* state in terms of its relations with international law, i.e., a state where international law, whether in the terms of international customary law or of international conventions which Sweden has ratified, does not take effect within the national legal system without a special act of transformation that turns them into domestic law.[148] During the 1980s, however, the two highest Swedish courts gradually came to consider the ECHR as an important source of interpretation and inspiration.[149] Swedish laws were thus interpreted in the light of the convention and the case law from the Strasbourg court.[150]

256. The next step in the development came in 1994, when it was decided that when joining the EU, Sweden should also incorporate ECHR into national law. (Similar measures were simultaneously introduced in the other Nordic countries.) The incorporation took effect from 1 January 1995.[151] This was of course not coincidental; by incorporating ECHR at the same time that Sweden was going to join

148. From a legal point of view, this fact, in relation to ECHR, was acknowledged in two cases in the early 1970s from the Supreme Court and the Supreme Administrative Court respectively; see NJA 1973, p. 423 and RÅ 1974, p. 121.
149. For a general comment, see I. Cameron, An Introduction to the European Convention on Human Rights, 5th ed., Uppsala 2006, p. 153 ss.
150. See e.g., cases NJA 1988, p. 572, 1989, p. 131, 1990, p. 636, 1991, pp. 188 and 512, as well as RÅ 1990, ref. 75 and note 492.
151. The travaux préparatoires are to be found in the Governmental Bill (SOU) 1993:40, Parts A and B.

the EU, situations where the Convention would be applied or not depending on whether EU law was applicable were avoided.[152]

257. However, the incorporation nevertheless took place in a problematic way, in particular from a legal point of view. Due to a political compromise, the ECHR, despite being referred to in former IG Chapter 2, Article 23 (now Chapter 2, Article 19) was not given constitutional status, but is as such incorporated through an ordinary law.[153] IG 2:19 simply states that 'No act of law or other provision may be adopted' which contravenes Sweden's undertakings under the ECHR. Thus, this may be seen as a rule directed to the legislator rather than the courts,[154] an impression that is strengthened by the fact that since ECHR is incorporated as an ordinary law, the restrictions and limitations on judicial review imposed by IG 11:14 apply with even greater force in relation to ECHR than in relation to the national constitution(s).[155] The situation, should a law passed either before or after 1 January 1995 be in conflict with the ECHR, was in the *travaux préparatoires* handed to the courts to deal with by the use of ordinary means of interpretation (e.g., rules on *lex posterior* and *lex specialis*).

258. What does this mean in practice, then? It could of course be seen to indicate that when a conflict, which is not manifest, will arise between the ECHR and a Swedish law or ordinance, the law or ordinance shall be applied.[156] But on the other hand, it must be noted that in the *travaux préparatoires*, both from the government and the Constitutional Committee of the Parliament, mentioning is made of the 'special character' and status of ECHR, which ought to give it a certain weight of its own in future conflicts with domestic laws (or ordinances).[157] On the basis of those remarks, Swedish courts ought to be able to find at least some room for *manoeuvering* if they want to secure the respect (if not supremacy) of ECHR.

259. Still, which is perhaps not entirely surprising against this background, the Swedish courts have so far been reluctant to use the ECHR, at least when this would mean setting aside a national law. In one case from 1998,[158] the Supreme Court even refused to uphold the Convention (as well as the FSA) against a demand from

152. The difference that the applicability of EU law may in fact have in a given case was however shown in the crucial *Lassagård* case from 1997 (RÅ 1997, ref. 65), which was decided in a totally different way by the Supreme Administrative court, setting a Swedish law aside, than a previous case (Stallknecht, NJA 1994, p. 657 and RÅ 1995, ref. 58) which concerned issues arising before Sweden's entry into the EU.
153. The number of which is 1994:1500.
154. Cfr Cameron, *supra*, p. 155 ss, as well as Bernitz, European Law in Sweden, p. 81 ss (Ch. 5 of the book, which is called The Incorporation of the European Human Rights Convention into Swedish Law – A half Measure).
155. For some recent remarks on this issue, taking new jurisprudence into account, see A. Bohlin/W. Warnling-Nerep, Förvaltningsrättens grunder, Stockholm 2004, p. 334 s.
156. Of course, it shall also be noted that the similarities between ECHR and Ch. 2 IG, which contains a rights catalogue, are striking. The main difference is that the protection of personal integrity and family life (Art. 8 ECHR) is definitely weaker in the Swedish constitution(s), given not least the wide right to access to documents in Sweden.
157. Prop 1993/94:117, p. 37 s as well as KU 1993/94:24, p. 19 s.
158. NJA 1998, p. 817.

Swedish and Norwegian authorities to execute a penal judgment from a Norwegian court (which was all the more embarrassing since Norway was six months later condemned by EctHR for violating the ECHR concerning that same issue).[159] At the same time, both the highest courts have been very clear in terms of acknowledging e.g., the impact of the principle of proportionality, flowing from ECHR.[160]

260. In the last few years, questions related to administrative tax sanctions (or penalties) and the possibility for Swedish courts to impose damages when the Convention has been violated have been in the focus of the discussion.[161] In both areas, it seems clear that while EctHR has found that certain violations of ECHR had taken place in Sweden, Swedish courts have been slow or even reluctant to take the full consequences of those judgments and come to the same conclusions as the EctHR did in almost identical cases.[162]

261. However, the Supreme Court in two rulings in June and July 2013 based on the *ne bis in idem* principle made a U-turn in its approach to imposing a tax surcharge on a person and prosecuting the same person for a tax offence in different legal proceedings.[163] In the first ruling, a unanimous plenary ruling in June 2013,[164] the Supreme Court found that the traditional Swedish double sanction system (tax surcharge and criminal sentence), applying two different legal procedures for providing false information in a tax declaration, was not compatible with the *ne bis in*

---

159. *Bladet Tromsö and Stensaas v. Norway*, case 21980/93, Reports 1999 p. The case concerned Norwegian fishermen who had publicly criticized methods used in the hunting of seal. For this, they were condemned to penalties by Norwegian courts, which in the case before EctHR was considered to be a violation of their freedom of speech (Art. 10 ECHR). The Swedish case concerned a fisher, Odd Lindberg, who had made such critical comments in a TV program which was later broadcasted in Sweden (and thus also seen in Norway, where almost everyone is able to watch Swedish TV). He was therefore also sentenced to a fine by a Norwegian court. The Norwegian authorities then pursued him, after he had taken refuge to Sweden, eager to have the penalty imposed. They were then helped in their work by the Swedish authorities and the Supreme Court could not find that the ECHR prevented those from executing the fine in Sweden (despite the fact that under the Freedom of Speech Act, the editor of the TV program and not Lindberg himself was legally responsible for any comments made in the program). Neither the FSA, nor the ECHR was thus upheld by the Swedish Supreme Court. From at least two points of view (and maybe also considering so-called *ordre public* in private international law), therefore, this judgment must be considered as a clear error.
160. See e.g., besides the cases referred to above, the case NJA 2001, p. 409.
161. For an overview of the early discussion, see Jan Södergren in Europarättslig tidskrift 2002, pp. 659–682.
162. The procedure for imposing administrative tax sanctions (*skattetillägg*) has been found by EctHR to be contrary to Art. 6 ECHR in the Cases *Janosevic and Västberga Taxi/Vulic v. Sweden*, 34619 and 36985/97, judgment 23 Jul. 2002, Reports 2002 p.
163. The literature on the subject is now becoming comprehensive. See in English case comment on Åkerberg Fransson by E. Hancox in CMLRev 2013 p. 1411 ff., D. Sarmiento, *Who's Afraid of the Charter?*, CMLRev (2013) pp. 1267 ff.; S. Peers et al. (eds), The *EU Charter of Fundamental Rights. A Commentary* (Oxford, 2014), pp. 1385 ff., pp. 1419 ff.; C. Brokelind, *Case Note on Åkerberg Fransson (Case C-617/10)*, European Taxation 53, no. 6 (2013) on the general background B. Van Bockel, *The Ne Bis in Idem Principle in EU Law* (Kluwer NL 2010), A.-I. Kargopoulos, *Ne bis in idem in Criminal Proceedings, Swedish Studies in European Law*, vol. 5 (Oxford, 2014), pp. 85 ff.
164. NJA (Nytt Juridiskt Arkiv) 2013 p. 502 (the Supreme Court's publication of decisions).

idem principle. It is clear that this important change in the Swedish legal position was brought about by the decision of the Court of Justice in the *Åkerberg Fransson* case in 2013.[165]

262. Later, in a follow-up ruling in July 2013,[166] the Supreme Court established that as a consequence of the recent change in the law, a person has the right to a new trial if he or she has paid a tax surcharge and in addition been sentenced in a criminal procedure for tax offence. The Supreme Court set the break off point for the right to use this extraordinary legal remedy to the 10 February 2009, the date when the European Court of Human Rights issued its important judgment in the *Zolotukhin* case.[167] In short, Zolotukhin clarified that the ne bis in idem principle in ECHR law prohibits a new prosecution or trial of an offence when it arises from identical facts or substantially the same facts as the first offence already prosecuted or tried.

263. These two rulings by the Supreme Court proved very quickly to have dramatic practical importance. In the following months a huge number of persons were released from prison where they were serving sentences for tax offences and many ongoing tax offence prosecutions were terminated. In all these cases, the convicted persons had to pay a tax surcharge.

264. The issue whether it was legally possible under ECHR to apply separate legal proceedings for tax surcharge and tax offences based on the same information in a tax return had been debated by Swedish lawyers for a long time. In 2002, the ECtHR had concluded in two cases that the Swedish system with tax surcharges was criminal in nature.[168] However, the decisions by the ECtHR did not lead to any change in the Swedish legislation. Neither did the courts change their practice. Obviously, the legislator wanted the taxation system to be enforced by sharp sanctions, Sweden being a country with high taxes. The lack of action by the legislator is thus best explained by pure economical reasons.

265. However, the new definition of what constitutes *ne bis in idem* in the Zolotukhin judgment in 2009 made the problem urgent. The Supreme Court ruled on the matter in two new decisions in 2010–2011. In the 2010 decision, which focused on the ECHR law, the majority of the justices took the view the Zolotukhin judgment did not give 'clear support' to the need to change Swedish practice.[169] This might be seen as an attempt to prevent an expansion of judicial review of legislation by Swedish courts, given that the previous requirement for 'manifest error' in IG Chapter 11, Article 14 was going to be abolished by 1 January 2011, as explained above.

165. C-617/10, Judgment 26 Feb. 2013 (ECR 2013:105).
166. NJA 2013 p. 746.
167. App. No. 14939/03, *Zolotukhin v. Russia*, judgment 10 Feb. 2009.
168. *Janosevic v. Sweden*, App. No. 34619/97 and *Västberga Taxi and Vulk v. Sweden*, App. No, 36985/97.
169. NJA 2010 p. 168.

266. In the 2011 case,[170] the defendant invoked the ne bis in idem principle in Article 50 of the Charter of Fundamental Rights. The case dealt partly with tax surcharges for undeclared VAT. A Supreme Court majority, three Supreme Court justices, concluded that the Swedish legal provisions on tax offences and tax surcharges lay outside the scope of the Charter, and that no preliminary ruling was thus required. Two dissenting justices took a different view and found that the legal position was not clear concerning the possible applicability of the Charter and that a preliminary ruling should thus be requested. In reality, the Supreme Court thus voted on whether a preliminary ruling should be requested by the Court of Justice or not. As is well-known, according to Article 267 TFEU (Treaty on the Functioning of the European Union), the highest instance is obliged to request a preliminary ruling if a case pertains to EU law, unless the legal position is clear (*acte clair*). Obviously, the Supreme Court did not observe that obligation, which was even more regrettable since the Court of Justice at that time had not clarified its position on the scope of the Charter. In its *Åkerberg Fransson* judgment, the Court of Justice found it necessary to include a reminder – obviously addressed to the Supreme Court – about the duty to observe Article 267 TFEU as interpreted in the CILFIT case.[171] In fact, given this obligation for Supreme Courts in 267 and the scope of the well-known CILFIT criteria, including the meaning of 'acte clair', a decision like this, refusing to ask for a preliminary ruling with three votes against two, can only be described as manifestly wrong, or even self-contradictory.

267. In Sweden, decisions from the Supreme Court are not formally binding on judges in lower courts. Still, they are almost all the time observed and followed. However, in this case, some judges in lower courts found the position taken by the Supreme Court clearly wrong and refused to follow it. This much observed 'revolt' among Swedish judges forms an important part of the background to the *Åkerberg Fransson* case, in which a district court *judge* in a small town, Haparanda in the very north of the country, decided to question the established Swedish system by asking the Court of Justice for a preliminary ruling.[172]

268. As far as economic compensation for violations of the convention is concerned, Swedish courts have tended, until 2005, when a new important case was decided as explained in §2 below, to view this as an exclusive competence of the EctHR, though this is in fact not quite in line with the case-law of that court, nor with the ECHR itself.

269. At the same time, however, ECHR is regularly being invoked and applied in a number of criminal law cases, not least in relation to the procedures applied. Thus, the picture is mixed and it seems too early to make a full evaluation of how ECHR is being dealt with by Swedish courts. While waiting for that, it may be noted

170. NJA 2011 p. 444.
171. Case 283/81, *Cilfit and Others* [1982] ECR 3415, para. 47 in the Åkerberg Fransson judgment.
172. See in particular O. Zetterquist, Strasbourg, Luxembourg – we have a problem – Reflektioner om ett litet HD-uppror, Festskrift till Pär Hallström (Reflections on a minor Supreme Court Rebellion, Festschrift in Honour of Pär Hallström) (2012): pp. 353 ff.

that a number of new monographic studies on the topic reveal a considerable interest in it from law scholars.[173] And the tendency is definitely clear, that the courts are becoming ever more interested in giving ECHR priority before regular national laws.

§2. The Catalogue of Human Rights in Chapter 2 of the Instrument of Government

I. Background and Structure

270. The old Swedish constitution of 1809 contained one single Article relating to human rights, namely its § 16 that in particular, in a very old-fashioned language, protected the right to a fair trial, the right to property and the freedom of religion. Still, at least in the twentieth century, both the legislative and the executive bodies showed that they in practice respected also many other fundamental rights, which was one of the reasons why, when the idea of a new constitution was started to being discussed in the 1950s and onwards, the introduction of a modern catalogue or Bill of Rights into such a document gradually gained more and more attention. Finally, those discussions led to the enactment of Chapter 2 of the IG, which has been modernized in 1976, 1979 and 1994 (notably with the inclusion of ECHR into the text).

271. The structure in Chapter 2 is based on the difference between *absolute* rights, which may never be restricted, and *relative* rights that may be restricted as explained below. Regardless of under which category a certain right will fall, it is important to note that Chapter 2 in its entirety consists of binding legal rules, as opposed to Chapter 1, Article 2 IG, which simply enumerates certain general aims for the activities of the public sector, as explained above in Part I.[174]

272. According to the traditional Swedish constitutional terminology, Chapter 2 IG contains four types of rights rules, namely so-called *positive freedoms of opinion*

---

173. See apart from the highly respected standard comment by Hans Danelius, Mänskliga rättigheter i europeisk praxis: en kommentar till Europakonventionen om de mänskliga rättigheterna, Stockholm 2002 also two dissertations on the right to property from recent years; Karin Åhman, Egendomsskyddet – Äganderätten enligt artikel 1 första tilläggsprotokollet till den Europeiska konventionen om de mänskliga fri-och rättigheterna, Uppsala 2000 and Gudrun Gauksdottir, The Right to Property and the European Convention on Human Rights – A Nordic Approach, Lund 2004. Judge Danelius also contributes regular comments on the case law of EctHR to the periodical Svensk Juristtidning.

174. Alongside Ch. 2, Art. 21, which mentions that all children covered by compulsory schooling shall be entitled to a free basic education at a public school and that the public institutions shall also be responsible for the provision of higher education, Ch. 1, Art. 2 is actually the only rule in the Swedish constitution that mentions any social, economic or cultural right. In other words, those rights are thus not as well protected in Swedish law as many foreigners probably think, which may historically be explained by the combined historical fact that the Social Democrats have always been sceptical to the constitutional enforcement and protection of rights in general, while the right-wing parties, who have favoured this, have not been very positive to social, economic and cultural rights as such, but rather to traditional, 'negative' or individual-based and thus in a way 'liberal' rights and freedoms.

(freedoms of speech, information, assembly and others) in Article 1, *negative freedoms of opinion* (the right not to be forced to make statements or participate in meetings and other activities), which are to be found in Articles 2–3, the *physical rights and freedoms* in Articles 4–8 and finally a group of rule of law-related procedural guarantees in Articles 9–11. The Chapter does however also contain rules on to what extent it is possible for the legislator to restrict the rights in the first eleven Articles, which are to be found in Articles 20–24, as well as a general protection, for all legislation, against various forms of discrimination in Articles 12–13, a few rights with a very weak protection in Articles 14–18 (including right to property and intellectual property), the complicated regulation of the enactment of the ECHR in Article 19 and finally a detailed regulation of which rights that are valid also for foreigners in Article 25.

273. The most detailed knowledge of which rights that are absolute or possible to restrict is to be found in Chapter 2, Article 20, section 1 IG but in fact, not even that Article reveals the whole truth on this matter. Instead, it is actually easier to analyse the different rights one by one in order to grasp their content and reach, and then discuss issues related to their possible restriction.

II. The Individual Rights

274. The first individual right to be mentioned in Chapter 2 is the freedom of expression (Article 1, section 1, point 1), which is there defined as the freedom to communicate information and express thoughts, opinions and sentiments, whether orally, pictorially, in writing or in any other way. Since such freedom is protected by FPA and FSA when exercised in different medias, it goes without saying that only a limited field of freedom of speech is actually left to be protected 'only' by the IG; what remains is basically opinions, utterances or statements passed between individuals or in small groups, as well as the ones presented at theatre or art performances or at public meetings which are not showed in radio or TV (which are however also protected by the freedom of assembly).[175]

275. The freedom of information stands in a close connection to the freedom of speech and may even be described as its flip-side.[176] It is in Chapter 2, Article 1, section 1, point 2 described as the freedom to procure and receive information and otherwise acquaint oneself with the utterances of others, but it is worth underlining that it does not include the access of documents covered by Chapter 2 of the FPA, as emphasized by the last section of Chapter 2, Article 1 IG. Access to documents thus forms another kind of freedom of information, so to speak, all on its own.

276. The freedom of assembly and the freedom to demonstrate, Article 1, section 1, points 3–4, share a rather unitary regulation, since they cover very similar

175. See also Nergelius, *supra*, p. 118.
176. It is e.g., so described by prop 1975/76:209, at p. 110.

situations and may also be restricted for similar reasons.[177] Here, the police may be authorized to prevent, prohibit or stop and even dissolve meetings and demonstrations at public places, according to law, if it is necessary in light of the situation, the public order or the traffic.

277. When it comes to the freedom of association in Chapter 2, Article 1, section 1, point 5 IG, it protects the freedom to associate with others for private or public purposes, which includes associations that are mainly commercially oriented. This freedom may, under Chapter 2, Article 14, section 2 in fact only be restricted in respect of organizations whose activities are of military or quasi-military nature, or constitute persecution of a population group of a particular race, colour or ethnic origin. That requirement has in practice been interpreted as prohibiting racist organizations in general – a measure actually desired by the UN – which shows that this right as such is probably more difficult to restrict than most other rights in Chapter 2, Article 1, though it is not equally well protected as the freedom of religion, which is under Articles 20 and 23–24 *e contrario* literally not possible to limit at all. That is however hardly the case in reality, since it is not possible to invoke the freedom of religion e.g., in order to justify otherwise illegal actions. Normally, other rights would not enjoy a strengthened protection when they are exercised within a religious context, though that may now be doubted after the so-called *Reverend Green* case from 2005, which is further analysed below.[178] The more specific effect of the impossibility to limit the freedom of religion instead seems to be that such restrictions may never be directed against the exercise of *one single form* of religion or one specific creed.[179]

278. As mentioned above, citizens are also protected against having to reveal their opinions or engage themselves in various activities. According to Chapter 2, Article 2 IG, every citizen shall be protected in his relations with the public institutions against any coercion to divulge an opinion in a political, religious, cultural or other such connection, as well as protected 'in his relations with the public institutions' against any coercion to participate in a meeting for the formation of opinion or a demonstration or other manifestation of opinion, or to belong to a political association, religious community or other association for opinion referred to in sentence one. The freedom of association is undoubtedly the most controversial topic here, since this regulation does not as such protect individuals from not being obliged to be members of for instance a trade union, though that negative right

177. The main difference between them would otherwise seem to be that a demonstration or manifestation could be performed by one single person, while a meeting would seem to require the presence of at least three persons. It may also be held that a meeting directs its message inwards, to the participants themselves, while the demonstration seeks to catch the attention of the surrounding world. However, those distinctions are not very sharp and maybe not always so practically important.

178. NJA 2005, p. 805.

179. See *more* in detail Nergelius, *supra*, p. 121 ss.

seems to be covered under the ECHR.[180] The issue has been controversial in Swedish law for a long time and does also have a role in several pending proceedings before the courts both in Luxemburg and Strasbourg.

279. Furthermore, as far as this negative kind of protection is concerned, it shall be noted that under Chapter 2, Article 3 IG, no record in a public register concerning a citizen may without his consent be based solely on his political opinions.[181] This is however also a contested right, since it does obviously not apply in relation to private registers, like the ones that may be established by political parties over their adversaries and opponents. And even public registers may obviously be allowed if they contain just some additional piece of information, except notes on someone's political opinions. The protection, which does according to Chapter 2, Article 25 not at all apply to foreigners, is thus in fact not very strong at all.[182]

280. As far as the physical freedoms are concerned, prohibition against capital or corporal punishment or torture (Articles 4–5) is absolute, which is hardly surprising. The protection against other forms of physical violation, body and house searches and other invasions of privacy, against examination of mail or other confidential correspondence, eavesdropping and recording of telephone conversations or other confidential communications in Article 6 is on the other hand much more limited, since it may be restricted in law according to Article 20, section 1. In fact, this has also been one of the most controversial areas of legislation in recent years, due in particular to several, allegedly anti-terrorism measures that have occurred since 2001.

281. In the same manner, the prohibition in Chapter 2, Article 7 for Swedish citizens against deportation from or refusal of entry into the Realm is absolute,[183] while the freedom of movement and general protection of personal liberty in Chapter 2, Article 8 may be limited by law according to Article 12. Such laws, of which rules on criminal sanctions may be the most well-known, are in fact quite common. The protection for the citizenship in Chapter 2, Article 7 was severely strengthened by a judgment from the Supreme Court in April 2014, when a person who had been

---

180. See in Swedish law NJA 1982, p. 853, and in the jurisprudence of the Strasbourg court in particular the Case *Sigurdur A. Sigurjonsson v. Iceland*, Judgment 30 Jun. 1993, Series A, No. 264, where this kind of negative freedom of association seems to have been clearly acknowledged.

181. From s. 2 of that article, it also follows that every citizen shall be protected, to the extent set out in detail in law, against any violation of personal integrity resulting from the registration of personal information by means of automatic data processing. This rule is however not wider than the relevant, applicable legislation in that area will allow.

182. It may be noted that Sweden was on this or rather a similar point in ECHR condemned by the Strasbourg court in 2006, in the Case *Segerstedt-Wiberg et al. v. Sweden*, 62332/00, Judgment 6 Jun. 2006.

183. After a number of changes in recent years, it is now also more or less impossible for anyone to lose a Swedish citizenship, as follows from s. 2 of that Article. The rules on citizenship are dealt with by Hedvig Lokrantz-Bernitz in the extensive study Medborgarskapet i Sverige och Europa – Räckvidd och rättigheter, Stockholm 2004. The issue is also dealt with by Warnling-Nerep et al., *supra*, Ch. 8.

wrongly deprived of his Swedish citizenship was awarded a financial compensation of SEK 100,000.[184]

282. Concerning the more 'rule of law-related' procedural guarantees, the right of any citizen who is deprived of his liberty on account of a criminal act or suspension thereof – or for other reasons, according to section 2 – to have the matter examined before a court without undue delay in Chapter 2, Article 9 is absolute. The same goes for the protection against retroactive penal sanctions in Chapter 2, Article 10, section 1, while the protection against retroactive tax legislation in section 2 of that same Article is much more limited, as follows from the wording of the rule.[185] The prohibition against courts set up for particular cases in Chapter 2, Article 11, section 1 is absolute, while the requirement in section 2 of that Article that proceedings in courts shall be open to the public is relative (and in practice often limited). In that same section 2, a small adaptation in order to bring Swedish law more in line with Article 6 of the ECHR has been made in 2010.

283. The really weak rights within Chapter 2 are the ones mentioned in Articles 14–18. What those rules have in common is that they simply establish that citizens have certain rights according to existing law(s), rights that could consequently just as well be withdrawn or abolished through use of law.[186] This goes for intellectual property rights (IG 2:16) as well as the right of trade unions to use strikes as a weapon during conflicts (2:14). Of those rights, however, the most contested one, since a long time, is the right to property in Chapter 2, Article 15.[187]

284. While this Article, until 1 January 1995, simply referred to the existing law in order to determine where the limits of right to property were to be drawn, it does from that date start with a more principled announcement, which states that the property of every citizen shall be so guaranteed that none may be compelled by expropriation or other such disposition (an expression that covers situations where the owner is deprived also of immaterial, intellectual property rights or e.g., rights under a lease contract) to surrender property to the public institutions or to a private subject, or tolerate restrictions by the public institutions of the use of land or buildings, other than where this is necessary in order to satisfy pressing public interests. It does in other words protect the right to property, or ownership or peaceful enjoyment of one's possessions or whatever it may be called, in a way that was not envisaged before, although the need to take environmental law into account when the compensation is determined has been stressed in 2010.[188]

---

184. NJA 2014 p. 323.
185. In fact, it is thus surprising that this rule has been used by the courts in a number of judicial review cases, notably NJA 2000, p. 132, as will be explained in the next section.
186. In fact, the right to trade or professional activity in Ch. 2, Art. 20 is even weaker than that and simply mentions when and why restrictions in the right may be introduced.
187. Which does also, in its s. 3, contain a reference to the general access to the nature (so-called *allemansrätt*), the implications of which will not be dealt with here.
188. An interesting new case, strengthening the right to property, is NJA 2014 p. 332.

285. Alongside with that, also the right to financial compensation in the case of an intrusion into someone's property has been strengthened under Chapter 2, Article 15, section 2. According to that rule, which was also introduced in 1995, a person who is compelled to surrender property by expropriation or other such disposition shall be guaranteed compensation for his loss. Such compensation shall also be guaranteed to a person whose use of land or buildings is restricted by the public institutions in such a manner that ongoing land use in the affected part of the property is substantially impaired, or if an injury results that is significant in relation to the value of that part of the property; the compensation as such is then still to be determined according to principles laid down in law, while the number of situations giving rise to such compensation has been widely extended.[189]

III. The Range and Extent of the Rights

286. The question of the range of the various rights may be analysed from many different points of view, one of which is to what extent those rights do apply to foreigners. That issue is entirely regulated in Chapter 2, Article 25 IG. According to that rule, then, there are certain rights in relation to which foreigners are generally equated with Swedish citizens (not mentioned at all in the article) and others where this is the case unless otherwise is provided by law (enumerated in the article).

287. The second category contains all the positive opinion freedoms in Article 1, protection against coercion to divulge an opinion (Article 2, sentence one), protection against physical violations in other cases than those falling under Articles 4 and 5, against body and house searches and other such invasions of privacy and against violations of confidential communications (Article 6), protection against deprivation of liberty (Article 8, sentence one), the right to have another deprivation of liberty than on account of a criminal act or the suspicion thereof examined before a court of law (Article 9, sections 2–3), the right to public court proceedings (Article 11, section 2), protection against interventions on grounds of opinion (Article 12, section 2, 3rd sentence),[190] intellectual property rights (Article 16) and finally the right to trade or practice a profession in Article 17.

288. Any law that may differ between Swedish citizens and foreigners shall in accordance with section 2 of Article 25 be subject to a special procedure for the enactment of certain laws that limit at least some of the basic rights in Chapter 2, which is to be found in Chapter 2, Articles 20–24.

289. The conditions or requirements for such limitations are to be found in section 2 of Chapter 2, Article 22, which applies to all kind of restrictions, and

189. The main question, once this new rule has been introduced, is undoubtedly what the expression 'pressing public interests' really means. According to the law bill, it may cover e.g., the need to protect the environment, or a need to build houses or streets; in other words, the expression is (deliberately) vague and possible to invoke in many situations.
190. The rules in Ch. 2, Arts 12–14 as well as 15–16 will be dealt with more in detail below.

Articles 23–24, which apply, with further criteria for restrictions, in relation to the specific positive freedoms of opinion mentioned there. First of all, then, we must observe that those rights that may be limited at all may only be so through law, under Chapter 2, Article 20, section 1, 1st sentence, [191] with some few, not so practically important exceptions that are also mentioned in the Article. And according to Article 21 such restrictions may only be imposed to satisfy a purpose that is acceptable in a democratic society. They must never go beyond what is necessary having regard to the purpose which occasioned it, nor may they be carried so far as to constitute a threat to the free formation of opinion as one of the fundaments of democracy or be imposed solely on grounds of a political, religious, cultural or other such opinion.

290. Those general requirements are then further qualified, as far as the positive freedoms of opinion are concerned, in Articles 23–24. Thus, the freedom of expression and information may, under Article 23, be restricted having regard to the security of the Realm, the national supply of goods, public order and safety, the good name of the individual, the sanctity of private life, and the prevention and prosecution of crime. Freedom of expression may also be restricted in commercial activities, which is hardly strange, but on top of that, those two freedoms may always be restricted 'where particularly important grounds so warrant', a reason for restriction that has always been controversial.[192] For all those kinds of restrictions the same criteria applies, namely that particular regard shall be had to the importance of the widest possible freedom of expression and information in political, religious, professional, scientific and cultural matters (Article 13, section 2).

291. Freedom of assembly and demonstration may under Chapter 2, Article 24, section 1 be restricted in the interests of preserving public order and safety at a meeting or demonstration, or having regard to the circulation of traffic (!), with regard to the security of the Realm or in order to combat an epidemic. Under section 2 of that same Article, freedom of association may be restricted only in respect of organizations whose activities are of a military or quasi-military nature or who persecute population groups of particular race, colour or ethnic origin. This means that generally racist organizations may not be prohibited as such, simply because of their ideas, which has for a long time been a much debated issue.

292. Those are the material requirements for restrictions, so to speak. The formal requirements, on the other hand, are to be found in Chapter 2, Article 22. Those rules state that a draft law restricting one of the rights mentioned in Article 12, section 1, or a proposal for the amendment or abrogation of such a law, unless rejected shall be held in abeyance for at least twelve months from the date on which the first committee report on it was submitted to the Chamber, if so moved by at least 10 MP's, unless the proposal is supported by at least five sixths of those MP's voting (in which case it will enter into force immediately). In other words, a

191. See in this respect also Ch. 8, Art. 1 IG.
192. See *further* Nergelius, *supra*, p. 136 ss.

minority of one sixth of the MP's may always assure that a proposal of this kind will 'rest' or be held in abeyance for one year, which is not unimportant.[193]

293. The rule has so far been applied on nine different occasions, the first one in 1981 concerning prohibition of violent video cassettes, a few ones in the late 1980s concerning a law on foreigners and espionage against companies, which was perceived to limit the rights of informants or 'whistleblowers', and then in a few more cases concerning conditions for broadcasting of commercial radio.[194] Interestingly enough, the provision was used again in the spring of 2006 concerning a proposal for increased surveillance by wiretapping or eavesdropping, and was in 2007 once again invoked in a similar case concerning electronic messages, which shows that it has some importance, though there is yet no example of any restrictive law actually being stopped through the use of it. It is also a fact that in all the cases where it has been invoked (Most recently concerning implementation of the EU data directive into Swedish law in 2011[195]), the political differences in opinion have remained one year later, when the proposal came up for decision in the Chamber once again. Its importance shall thus not be overestimated.

294. Apart from all those formal matters, it must be emphasised that the scope and extent of the IG and its chapter on rights was very much strengthened due to two judgments on 23 April 2014, when financial compensation was awarded due to violations of the right to citizenship and the right to property.[196]

§3. THE FREEDOM OF PRESS ACT

295. While the old constitution of 1809 contained one single Article relating to human rights (its §16, as mentioned above), the freedom of speech exercised in books and journals (i.e., in printed works, a fact that is revealed in the ancient, original but still existing Swedish title of the Freedom of Press Act, Tryckfrihetsförordningen) has been constitutionally protected ever since 1766.[197] Until 1 January 1992, when the Freedom of Speech Act entered into force, the current Freedom of Press Act from 1949 was analogously applied also on other media than books and journals, for which it is really intended. Historically, the only way to explain this somewhat privileged and internationally very unusual position of the printed word

193. Since it may sometimes be hard to decide when a draft law does really constitute a restriction of a basic right, s. 5 of Art. 12 states that the Committee on the Constitution will determine that on behalf of the Parliament. According to the Riksdag Act Ch. 4, Art. 11, s. 3, the Committee may not declare that a draft law does *not* constitute such a restriction without obtaining the opinion of the Law Council on the matter, but the Committee is then not bound to follow the opinion of the Law Council.
194. See for a detailed account Nergelius, *supra*, p. 144 ss.
195. See JuU 2011/12:28 and KU 2010/11:3y.
196. NJA 2014 pp. 323 and 332.
197. After an interruption from 1772, a new Freedom of Press Act was enacted in 1810 and then modified in 1812. When that one was perceived to have been misused or even abused by the authorities under the Second World War, a new one (the current, still existing one) was adopted in 1949. To print something is in Swedish thus called 'trycka'.

within the constitutional regulation of the country is undoubtedly an awareness of the importance that books and journals have always had in the formation of opinions (and the importance of access to documents and transparency within the administration in order to combat corruption and misuse of power). Since TV and other media have a similar position today, the enactment of the Freedom of Speech Act in 1992 is also logical from this point of view.

296. According to Chapter 1, Articles 5–6 of the FPA, the Act applies to all written matter produced with a printing press, provided that certain formal and technical conditions are fulfilled.[198] It does however not apply to every word that is to be found in such material. As stated above, there are now three kinds of freedom of speech in Swedish constitutional law, namely the ones covered respectively by the IG, the FPA and the FSA, while at the same time a certain kind of statements or utterances do by definition fall outside all those three acts, namely the ones that are simply criminal, for instance because they are a part of a fraud or some other crime. Certain other limitations of the strengthened protection of freedom of speech that FPA does indeed provide are also envisaged by its Chapter 1, Article 9, in particular in relation to commercial advertising.[199]

297. Certain important definitions of what freedom of press means are found already in Chapter 1, Article 1 FPA. Thus, the freedom of the press is defined in Chapter 1, Article 1, section 1 as the right of every Swedish citizen to publish written matter, without prior hindrance by any public authority, and not to be prosecuted thereafter on grounds of its content other than before a lawful court (using a special jury system, as explained below), or punished therefore other than because the content contravenes an express provision of law. Perhaps even more important is section 2 of the same Article, according to which, in order to secure the free exchange of opinion and availability of comprehensive information, every Swedish citizen shall be free, subject to the rules in FPA, to express his thoughts and opinions in print, to publish official documents and to communicate information and intelligence on any subject whatsoever (so-called *meddelarfrihet*, which is wide and internationally very unusual).[200]

298. In line with this, no scrutiny of any written matter prior to printing may exist according to Chapter 1, Article 2, which also states that no actions not authorized under the FPA are allowed for the authorities in order to prevent the printing, publication or dissemination of written matter on grounds of its content.[201] Chapter

198. In this respect, see also Ch. 1, Art. 7.
199. While such advertising that does also contain some message of an ideological or other kind does normally, according to settled jurisprudence, fall within the scope of FPA. Further limitations are made in relation to rules on copyright and intellectual property, Ch. 1, Art. 8, as well as child pornography, Ch. 1, Art. 10.
200. According to Ch. 7, Art. 3, it does however not apply in relation to some very serious crimes such as espionage and deliberate disregard of a duty of confidentiality.
201. See also Ch. 1, Art. 3, which states that no person may be prosecuted or held liable under penal law or subject to other sanctions on account of an abuse of the freedom of the press other than as prescribed by the FPA.

1, Article 4 contains the so-called *instruction*, which judges and jurors are supposed to observe when passing judgment on abuses of the freedom of the press. This Article states that they should then constantly bear in mind the connection between the freedom of the press and its role in a free society, direct attention 'always more to illegality of subject matter and thought than to illegality of expression, to the aim rather than the manner of presentation', and, in case of doubt, acquit rather than convict.

299. Thus, there is no lack within Chapter 1 of FPA of general, principled statements in favour of and aiming at protecting the freedom of expression. But in its remaining Chapters 2–14, the emphasis is on criminal, procedural and even some civil law rules. Thus, the freedom to print and disseminate printed works is protected through Chapter 4, section 1 and Chapter 6, section 1 FPA,[202] while the freedom of information is protected, except through the rules on access to documents in the lengthy Chapter 2 and the special secrecy act,[203] also through rules on the right to anonymity in Chapter 3. Thus, under Chapter 3, Article 1, an author of printed matter or a person who has communicated information shall not be obliged to have his name or pseudonym set out therein. Furthermore, according to Chapter 3, Article 2, it shall not be permitted to inquire into the identity of an author or a person who has communicated information in a case relating to an offence against the freedom of the press, nor to inquire into the identity of the editor of non-periodical printed matter.[204] Similarly, a person who has been active in the production or publication of printed matter, or in an enterprise for the publication of such matter, or an enterprise that professionally purveys news or other material to periodicals, may not disclose what has come to his knowledge in this connection concerning the identity of an author or a person who has communicated information.[205] Thus, a system with so-called 'whistleblowers', to use a modern word, may be said to be constitutionally protected in Sweden (though the system has deeper historical roots than that expression may indicate).[206]

300. Foreigners are in principle equal with Swedes concerning the interpretation and application of the rules of FPA, as follows from Chapter 14, Article 5, section 2. The Act itself, however, contains a number of important rules which do reserve certain rights, i.e., to print and disseminate printed matter (Chapters 4, Articles 1 and

202. See in this respect also Ch. 5, Arts 4–7.
203. Offentlighets- och Sekretesslagen, 2009:400. According to FPA Ch. 2, s. 1, every Swedish citizen shall be entitled to have free access to official documents, in order to encourage the free exchange of opinion and the availability of comprehensive information. That right may be restricted for certain purposes enumerated in Ch. 2, Art. 2, after which follow, in the rest of the Ch. (Arts 3–18) a number of definitions of what is and what is not a document.
204. Only if, where non-periodical printed matter is concerned, the author or editor has been identified on the publication by name, or by means of a pseudonym or pen-name known generally to refer to a particular person, or if a person has acknowledged in a written statement that he is the author or editor, or has voluntarily made such a declaration before a court of law during the case, may the question of whether he is liable be considered during the proceedings.
205. The same rules apply also for editors of non-periodical printed matter.
206. Certain exceptions from this protection of anonymity are enumerated in Ch. 3, Art. 3, s. 2, pp. 1–5, which cover some rather special situations and shall not deter attention from the main rule.

6, Article 1) to Swedish citizens, which may be doubtful from an EU law perspective. Against that background, an important rule was introduced in 1994 in Chapter 5, Article 1, according to which it may be provided in law that also a foreign national or foreign legal person may be the owner of a Swedish periodical publication. Still, it seems doubtful whether the act in its entirety is compatible with EU law.

301. Those doubts do however not include the special liability rules in Chapter 8, which follow after a lengthy enumeration of which crimes that are punishable under the FPA, i.e., when they are committed through a written work, in Chapter 7 (notably its Articles 4–5).[207] The liability rules are based on the idea that *one person may always be held to be responsible*, be it the editor, the author or someone else and that in this 'chain of responsibility' thus established, if one, primarily liable person may not be found, the responsibility will pass over to someone else. The rules are different for periodicals as compared to non-periodicals; in the first category, the responsible editor at the time when the periodical was published (the criteria of whom are determined in Chapter 5) is normally responsible under Chapter 8, Article 1. This means in practice that if a case is brought against that periodical, the responsible editor (*ansvarig utgivare*) goes before the court and tries to defend the actions of the paper.[208] However, if such an editor has not been properly appointed, the liability passes over to the owner of the paper,[209] Chapter 8, Article 2, and if his identity may not be established either, it passes over to the printer, Chapter 8, Article 3. In case the periodical does not properly reveal where it has been printed, it will finally pass over to the disseminator under Chapter 8, Article 4.

302. For non-periodicals, i.e., books on the other hand, the liability lies primarily with the author under Chapter 8, Article 5, unless he has decided to remain anonymous in accordance with Chapter 3, Article 2 or if it is otherwise clear that the matter has been published without his consent or if his name or pseudonym appears in the book against his will. In that case, liability will pass to the editor, Chapter 8, Article 6, who may however also avoid responsibility in certain peculiar situations,[210] in which cases the publisher will be liable under Chapter 8, Article 7. If a publisher may not be identified, responsibility will pass to the printer and ultimately to the disseminator under Articles 8–9.

303. In any case, once a responsible person is identified, criminal proceedings will start under a court in accordance with Chapter 12 FPA. The Chancellor of Justice or someone he has appointed is normally the prosecutor on behalf of the State, though in libel cases it is more usual that persons who feel badly wounded bring actions themselves. Actions will be heard by a district court with a special competence in that kind of cases, Chapter 12, Article 1. In all cases which involve a

207. This list ranges from high treason and espionage to agitation against a population group, defamation, unlawful threats and deliberate setting aside of a duty of confidentiality.
208. Normally, of course, he is then assisted by a professional lawyer.
209. Who is under Ch. 5, Art. 3 responsible for appointing the editor.
210. In fact, not all books have an editor, which means that the legal importance of this particular Article is not always very high.

question of liability under penal law, the question of whether an offence has been committed shall be tried by a jury of nine members, who will establish that an offence has taken place by a majority of six votes to three. However, if the jury finds that no offence has been committed, the defendant shall be acquitted. If the jury on the other hand finds that an offence has been committed, the question shall be examined also by the court, but if the opinion of the court differs from that of the jury, the court is still entitled to acquit the defendant or apply a penal provision carrying a milder sanction than that applied by the jury. A superior court to which the judgment of a district court has been referred on appeal is no more entitled than the district court to overturn the jury's verdict.

304. This is in fact the only situation in Swedish law where a jury is sitting.[211] The existence of this jury undoubtedly gives the defendant in freedom of press cases a strong legal position in the trial. Therefore, the jury system is indeed an important part of this particular area of Swedish law.[212]

§4. The Freedom of Speech Act

305. The content, structure and function of the Freedom of Speech Act[213] is in fact very similar to the Freedom of Press Act, which means that simple repetitions will be avoided here, if possible.[214] The background to the enactment of this new constitutional act has already been mentioned, but it may be stressed once again that it may historically seem strange that while the freedom of speech exercised in a certain form, i.e., through written words in printed works, was constitutionally protected ever since 1766, no other kind of freedom of speech was mentioned in any constitutional act until more than two centuries later, i.e., in 1974. And with the gradual technological development, that fact became even stranger, which led to the appointment of a number of governmental committees analysing the issue, before the Freedom of Speech was finally decided upon in 1991 and entered into force on 1 January 1992.

306. Which are the main differences, then, between FSA and FPA? According to Chapter 1, Article 1, section 1 of FSA, its aim is to guarantee every Swedish citizen vis-à-vis the public institutions the right publicly to express his thoughts, opinions and sentiments, and in general to communicate information on any subject whatsoever on sound radio, television and certain similar transmissions, films, video

211. Concerning appointment of the jury and similar issues, see Ch. 12, Arts 3–6.
212. The history and function of the jury has quite recently been studied by T. Vallinder in a huge biography called Nio edsvurna män: jury och tryckfrihet I Sverige 1815–2000, Stockholm 2000. See also G. Persson, Exklusivitetsfråga: om förhållandet mellan tryckfrihet, yttrandefrihet och annan rätt, Stockholm 2002.
213. Which in the official translation from the Swedish Parliament bears the long title The Fundamental Law on Freedom of Expression, which will however not be used here.
214. In fact, a governmental committee has very recently proposed to combine them in one single constitutional act; see SOU 2006: 96, Ett nytt grundlagsskydd för tryck- och yttrandefriheten. This reform does however not look likely to be realized in the foreseeable future.

recordings, sound recordings and other technical recordings. In other words, the highly technical nature of the act is revealed already here, though the following text talks mainly of radio programs (which according to Chapter 1, Article 1, section 3 do also, surprisingly enough, include TV programs), films and sound recordings. Also the purpose of the freedom of expression under the act is defined in a way which is very similar to FPA, though Chapter 1, Article 1, section 2 of FSA does also specifically mention the freedom of artistic creation.[215] If any difference between them is to be identified, it is probably that the number of persons protected by FSA could sometimes or even normally be larger, since it will normally include both the artist or producer of a work that is performed in some thus protected media (like the director of a film, the composer of a song or the writer of a play) and the performers (the singer, actors or the one who is being interviewed in a news program). This fact, which becomes evident when the rules are analysed, is however not mentioned in the text.[216]

307. As mentioned, the rules are very similar as to their content and meaning to the ones in FPA, though a few deviations shall here be mentioned. Thus, prior scrutiny and censorship is forbidden according to Chapter 1, Article 3, though provisions may still under its section 2 be laid down in law concerning the scrutiny and approval of moving pictures in films, video recordings or other technical recordings intended for public showing. Such prior scrutiny is thus still possible and in fact existing in Sweden, which may be slightly surprising.[217]

308. Concerning transmissions, a distinction is made in Chapter 3 between transmissions by landline, which are entirely free, and the right to transmit radio programmes through other means, which may be – and in fact is – regulated in an act of law containing provisions on licensing and conditions on transmission. This is of course particularly important as far as radio and TV programs are concerned, while other technical recordings may be produced and disseminated by anyone under Article 3, Chapter 8.[218]

215. Which may be justified by the fact that typical films and sound recordings will normally tend to have a limited impact on the formation of opinion.
216. A further difference is that the possibilities to restrict commercial broadcasting are more far-reaching under FSA, as follows notably from Ch. 1, Art. 12, s. 2. The issue is however technically very complicated and will therefore not be dealt with here.
217. In the more technical sphere, it should also be mentioned that public authorities may according to Ch. 1, Art. 3, s. 3 not prohibit or prevent the possession or employment of such technical aids as are necessary to receive radio programmes or comprehend the content of technical recordings on grounds of the content of a radio programme or technical recordings, or ban the construction of landmine networks for the transmission of radio programmes, except by virtue of FSA itself. In at least a principled way, this rule will further strengthen the freedom of information.
218. The text here only talks of Swedish citizens and legal persons, but as follows from Ch. 11, Art. 1, s. 3, foreign nationals are normally equated with Swedish citizens under FSA (though differences may be provided in law). – *A proposal for some modernizing changes in this act has been made through the bill 2009/10:81.*

Chapter 2. Judicial Review in Swedish Law

§1. Relation between Judicial Review and Judicial Preview

309. In order to understand the historically rather limited impact of judicial review in Swedish law, it is probably not enough to be aware of the heavy emphasis on popular sovereignty in Swedish political and constitutional thinking. Also the important work of the Law Council,[219] which has since 1909 exercised a kind of judicial preview in relation to law proposals, must be observed in this respect.[220]

310. According to Chapter 8, Article 20 IG, the Law Council, which consists of justices or former justices from the two Supreme Courts, shall pronounce opinions on draft legislation. The opinion of the Council is obtained by the Government or sometimes by a committee of the Riksdag.[221] In order to understand a little bit more how the Council works, Article 21 shall be quoted *in extenso* (in the official version, whatever we may think of it):

> An opinion of the Council is obtained by the Government or, in accordance with what is stated in the Riksdag Act, by a Parliamentary Committee.
> Such an opinion shall be obtained before the Parliament enacts
> *1.* A fundamental law relating to the freedom of the press or the corresponding freedom of expression on sound radio, television and certain like transmissions and certain like transmissions and technical recordings,
> *2.* an act of law restricting the right of access to official documents;
> *3.* an act of law under Chapter 2, Article 14-16, Article 20 or Article 25
> an act of law concerning automatised treatment of personally identified or classified information,
> an act of law relating to local taxation or a LWA which otherwise imposes duties on the municipalities;
> an act of law under Article 2 Section 1 p. 1 or 2[222] or an act of law under Chapter 11 or 12, or
> an act of law amending or abrogating any law under points 1-6 above.
> The foregoing does however not apply, if obtaining the opinion of the Council on Legislation would delay the handling of legislation in such a way that serious detriment would result. If the Government submits a proposal to the Riksdag for the making of an act of law in any matter referred to in sentence one, and there has been no prior consultation of the Council on Legislation, the Government shall at the same time inform the Riksdag of the reason for the omission. Failure to obtain the opinion of the Council on Legislation on a draft law never constitutes an obstacle to the application of the law.

---

219. Which is thus, in the official translation, called the Council of Legislation.
220. Thus, the creation of the Law Council stands in a close relation to the simultaneously installed Supreme Administrative Court, both reforms aiming at distributing the many tasks that the Supreme Court had under the old constitution of 1809 to some new bodies.
221. Which may then be done by a minority of five members of the committee under Ch. 4, Art. 11, s. 1 of the Riksdag Act, as explained above in Part II, Ch. 3.
222. That is of Ch. 8.

311. Further, also Chapter 8 Article 22 may be worth quoting, in order to get the full picture:

> The Council's scrutiny shall relate to:
> 1. the manner in which the draft law relates to the fundamental laws and the legal system in general;
> 2. the manner in which the different provisions of the draft law relate to one another;
> 3. the manner in which the draft law relates to the requirements of the rule of law;[223]
> 4. whether the draft law is so framed that the resulting act of law may be expected to satisfy the stated purposes of the proposed law;
> 5. what problems are likely to arise in applying the act of law.

312. There are a number of questions to be asked in relation to this provision. For instance, what does it mean that an opinion should be obtained? How important are the exceptions from that rule? And what do the general provisions in Article 22 on the emphasis of the scrutiny really mean?

313. What is probably more important than to analyse these and other parts of the provision in detail[224] is to observe the two main limitations of the power of the Council that should always be kept in mind, namely that, as clearly formulated in the Article, a failure to obtain an opinion from the Law Council will never constitute an obstacle to the application of the law. This fact could lead to the conclusion that the Council lacks importance, but that is hardly correct, as will be shown below.

314. In Swedish doctrine, the meaning of the criteria established in section 3 of the provision has been vividly discussed.[225] In short, there seems to be a general agreement that not only the text of the draft law but also its *travaux préparatoires* (that are in Swedish law normally quite important, as mentioned initially) must be taken into account. The survey of the Law Council must since 1995 also include the compatibility of a draft law with EU law and ECHR, which is one of the main reasons why the Law Council has ever since at least 2000 been so increasingly or even alarmingly critical against many new draft laws.[226]

315. While the criteria concerning how different provisions of the draft law relate to one another is mainly technical and normally not controversial, the mentioning in the text of the requirements of the rule of law (*rättssäkerhet*) has been much more contested, since it has led to a general discussion on when the survey may take account not only of strictly legal, but also of somewhat more political

223. This is actually the only provision in the Swedish Constitutional Acts where this expression is being used, which is worth observing.
224. For such a detailed analysis, see Nergelius, *supra*, p. 182 ss. See also R. Lavin, Lagrådet och den offentliga rätten 1999–2001, Lund 2001.
225. See Nergelius, *supra*, p. 185 ss with further references.
226. This tendency was observed and analysed in a sharp Article by the former member of the Council Judge Danelius, in Svensk Juristtidning 2004, pp. 25–33.

aspects of a draft law. In short, it may be noticed that the Law Council today obviously feels more free to criticize proposals also from this point of view, which may have something to do with a generally speaking lower quality in legislation today than twenty years ago, when the pressure to produce laws quickly was much less severe.[227]

316. That is however not to much use for the Law Council, when the Government and the Parliament are able to ignore its warnings (which is formally possible, since the opinions of the Law Council are never formally binding). The issue of which constitutional status that may be given or attributed to the opinions of the Council is still somewhat unclear. They are of course much more important than ordinary comments on legislation from NGO's or public authorities (*remisser*), since the Council is a body of legal expertise, which represents no party interests and, furthermore, comments on a draft law, i.e., a finished legislative product which the Government intends to submit to the Parliament, not merely on the work of a legislative committee or group of some kind.

317. In general, the Law Council does definitely not lack influence or ability to affect the final versions of the laws adopted by the Parliament.[228] Still, given the clear statements and formulations in Chapter 8, Articles 20-22, it would be impossible to claim that the opinion of the Law Council should have a higher status than a contradictory opinion of the Parliament, enacting a law despite Council's objections. But in such a case, which is far from unusual, the fact that the opinions of the Law Council have not been observed by the legislator may be one reason why it might be more natural and logical for a court to set the law aside in a subsequent case of judicial review.[229]

§2. The Development of Judicial Review: A Brief Historical Background

318. Judicial review did not become a part of the constitutional text until 1979, when Chapter 11, Article 14 IG was enacted. The sheer existence of judicial review has however been discussed in the legal doctrine at least since the 1880s. It may have been said to have been generally acknowledged by the doctrine in the 1930s circa, and finally accepted as a fact by the Supreme Court in a case in 1964.[230] After that, it was clear that the courts, but probably not other public authorities, could exercise judicial review, but it was also clear that they exercised this possibility with great self-restraint and that the requirement of manifest error for a law to be set aside – which actually may be traced back to a judgment from 1951[231] – was a part of this institute.

227. Cfr Danelius, *supra*.
228. Cfr Nergelius, *supra*, p. 194 ss for a recent analysis.
229. Cfr Nergelius, *supra*, p. 218 s.
230. NJA 1964, p. 471, concerning opening hours in shops (although that law was actually considered to be constitutional). For a thorough historical account, see Nergelius, *supra*, p. 198 ss.
231. NJA 1951, p. 39, as well as the case NJA 1948, p. 188.

319. After that judgment, the question of whether judicial review should be written into the constitution became a part of the huge reform work that was conducted before the new Constitution, the Instrument of Government, was finally adopted.[232] It was however not until 1979, in the second reform wave of the new constitution, that judicial review was finally written into the new constitutional text, and then not only with the reservations that follow from the requirement of manifest error but also with some influential political statements being made in some *travaux préparatoires*, notably from the Constitutional Committee, on the restraint from the courts that was necessary if this possibility for the courts should not gradually undermine the popular Swedish democracy.[233] But are those statements binding or equally influential today, almost thirty years later?

320. Chapter 11, Article 14, which was not changed between 1979 and 2010,[234] used to state that if a court or other public body finds that a provision conflicts with a rule of fundamental law or other superior statute, or finds that a procedure laid down in law has been disregarded in any important respect when the provision was made, the provision may not be applied; but if it has been approved by the Parliament or the Government, it shall be waived only if the error is manifest. Thus, judicial review pertains both to courts and other public authorities, a fact that in reality has probably diminished the importance of judicial review, since the public authorities will normally hesitate to engage themselves in such an activity, while the mentioning of them in the Article does not contribute in giving the courts any real feeling that this is their own, important task, so to speak.[235]

321. It is also clear from the wording of Chapter 11, Article 14 that the review exercised may be either formal or material to its nature. It is possible that the margin for the courts to exercise judicial review may be slightly greater in the formal cases, since they are politically perhaps more neutral. What is however not quite clear from the Article, or from the doctrine or jurisprudence, is whether the courts have an obligation to exercise judicial review whenever they may find such a situation in a case before them – which would also force them actively to look for such possible conflicts of norms – or if they may do so only when the argument is being

---

232. For details, see Nergelius, *supra*, p. 204 ss.
233. See in particular KU 1978/79:39 p. 13. The constitutional reforms during the 1970s and the reasons and political controversies behind them have been analysed in an important study by Algotsson, Medborgarrätten och regeringsformen from 1987.
234. But may on the other hand be changed in 2010, since that issue forms a part of the work of the Committee preparing a constitutional reform. A special study has for that very reason been produced by a group of experts in 2006; see *SOU 2007:85, Olika former av normkontroll.*
235. There are actually no signs at all of this idea in older doctrine or jurisprudence, which only dealt with judicial review exercised by the courts, until 1973, when the Minister of Justice apparently from nowhere came up with this idea (prop. 1973:90, p. 200), which has since then hardly been questioned, surprisingly enough. For an international point of view on this issue, we may refer to A.R. Brewer-Carìas, Judicial Review in Comparative Law, Cambridge 1992, p. 132: 'Theoretically, all public authorities and individuals could be entitled to inspect the irregularity of state acts and to consider whether the act is valid and obligatory. Since this would lead to juridical anarchy, positive law normally reserves this power to the judges.'

raised by the parties in a case.[236] Surprisingly enough, this issue has still not been resolved.

322. What is clear, however, is that there seems to exist no autonomous right to an *abstract* judicial review, independent of a specific case or dispute. This was actually established already in a case in 1987[237] and it has recently been confirmed by the ECJ in the *Unibet* case that EU law does not impose any specific conditions on the Member States in terms of allowing specific forms of judicial review, as long as effective remedies exist before independent courts of law.[238]

323. From jurisprudence, though not from the text itself, it also becomes clear, logically enough, that judicial review is not always exercised of a law or another rule in itself, but rather of the practical use or application of that rule that a public authority has made in a specific case.[239] In reality, judicial review would more or less have been impossible to use as an instrument for the courts had that not been the case.[240]

324. Concerning the requirement of manifest error, it may be surprising, not least from points of view of democracy and popular sovereignty, that the provisions passed by the Government (i.e., so-called regulations, *förordningar*) do enjoy the same degree of protection in this respect as the laws passed by the Parliament. The regulations from the Government do otherwise not enjoy the same constitutional status, as shown not least from Chapter 8 IG and furthermore, the Government is nowhere near being able to invoke democracy and the legitimacy that it contains as a force underlying its regulations in the same way as the Parliament may do.[241] Thus, if any kind of swift reforms should be envisaged in this area, an abolishment of the right of all the public authorities to exercise judicial review *and* of the manifest error condition in relation to acts of the Government would be two very suitable areas, that could probably be passed without major controversy.[242]

325. Against this background, it may of course be asked what the content and effect of Chapter 11, Article 14 really is, or perhaps rather what it was before 2010. Here, opinions are ranging from the fact that judicial review would actually have been stronger had the Article never been enacted[243] to the view that Chapter 11,

---

236. See Nergelius, *supra*, p. 210 for further discussion.
237. NJA 1987, p. 198.
238. Case C-432/05, Judgment 13 Mar. 2007, *ECR 2007 I p. 2271.*
239. For some very clear examples of this, see the two so-called *Kurd* cases, NJA 1989, p. 131 and 1990, p. 636. Also NJA 1986, p. 489 may be observed here.
240. For an analysis, see Nergelius, Förvaltningsprocess, normprövning och Europarätt, Stockholm (Norstedts) 2000 Ch. 6.
241. There are in fact certain examples of the two Supreme Courts showing less self-restraint in relation to regulations from the Government than when reviewing the constitutionality of laws; see e.g., RÅ 1993:10 and 79, as well as NJA 1996, p. 370. This tendency is however far from constant.
242. Incidentally, those are exactly the same changes that have been introduced in Finland; see Art. 106 of the Finnish Constitution from 2000.
243. An opinion somewhat surprisingly expressed by Bernitz, *supra.*

Article 14 is to such a high degree a product of the 1970s that it can hardly be interpreted literally today.[244] One major difficulty in that respect, apart from what was said above, is undoubtedly that the term 'manifest' (*uppenbar*) is so vague that it may mean different things to different persons. Thus, one leading, now retired professor and justice of the Supreme Court, Mr Bertil Bengtsson, has openly declared that the respect for the requirement may force him to uphold laws which he himself finds unconstitutional, as long as his learned colleagues have a different opinion. Also in practice, in two dissenting votes, has he shown his reluctance to set aside laws that his colleagues find valid, which undoubtedly illustrates some of the main problems with the rule.[245] One way to avoid such problems would be if Swedish judges frequently *interpreted* laws in a manner which made them consistent with the Constitution and European law, but studies devoted to that topic actually reveal that this has not been a frequent working method for Swedish courts.[246] Thus, the problem did not seem easy to remedy without a change of the Article itself.

326. But now that the rule has been changed, on the other hand, and the requirement of manifest error has thus finally been removed, the road should be open for Swedish courts to exercise judicial review much more often than before. Still, it is too early to predict what will really happen in this respect, but the current wording is this one:

> If a court finds that a provision conflicts with a rule of fundamental law or other superior statute, the provision shall not be applied. The same applies if a procedure laid down in law has been disregarded in any important respect when the provision was made.
> In the case of review of an act of law under paragraph one, particular attention must be paid to the fact that the Riksdag is the foremost representative of the people and that fundamental law takes precedence over other law.

§3. Some Important Cases

327. A rather thorough study on the development of Swedish judicial review between 1995–2002, which is particularly interesting since it covers the first seven years of Swedish EU membership, was presented in 2004 by the young scholar Karin Åhman, who had presented it first as an official report for the Ministry of Justice and then also published it in a constitutional anthology.[247] According to the

244. Most sharply by Nergelius, Svensk statsrätt.
245. Those are the two cases NJA 1981, p. 1 concerning rights of the Sami population (cfr today Ch. 2, Art. 20, s. 2 IG) and 1989, p. 131, concerning controversial restrictions in the freedom of movement for a group of Kurdish refugees.
246. See in particular Nergelius in Svensk Juristtidning 1996, pp. 835–870. For a slightly different view, see K. Åhman, Rättighetsskyddet i praktiken – skydd på papperet eller verkligt genomslag?, in O. Petersson/E. Smith (eds.), Konstitutionell demokrati, Stockholm 2004 (SNS), pp. 172–203.
247. *Ibid.* See also her more recent study from 2011, Normprövning – Domstols kontroll av svensk lags förenlighet med Regeringsformen och Europarätten 2000-2010.

somewhat official figures in that study, judicial review had been exercised by Swedish courts in 131 cases during that period, of which seventy-one were (finally) settled by the Supreme Court, thirty-eight from the Supreme Administrative Court and twenty-two are judgments from courts of appeals. In seventy of those cases, the courts found that no conflict between norms of a lower level and IG, ECHR or EU law had occurred.[248] No less than forty-eight cases were resolved by means of interpretation, which is actually somewhat surprising and contrary to a previous study from 1996.[249] Chapter 11, Article 14 were invoked in nine cases, of which the law or regulation was set aside in five. Apart from that, Swedish rules were set aside for being contrary to European law in three cases, but without that Article being explicitly invoked.

328. If we go even further back in history, we may note that quite a few cases have concerned the prohibition against retroactive tax laws in Chapter 2, Article 2, section 2. Those cases were initially rather technical to their nature, which perhaps made it easier for the courts to set aside some rules,[250] but in the case NJA 2000 s. 132, a law was explicitly set aside, surprisingly, for violating that rule. Generally speaking, however, it seems clear that technical rules like the ones in Chapter 8 IG have been easier for the courts to invoke against legislation that has not met certain formal requirements than material, crucial human rights rules like the ones in Chapter 2 IG or in ECHR:

> The examples of this in the jurisprudence are numerous, in particular from the Supreme Administrative Court. For instance, in the case RÅ 1980 1:92, that Court found that a law on the right of companies to make tax deduction for certain losses was found not to be general and thus not compatible with the former Chapter 11, Article 8 IG (now Chapter 11, Article 4). And in three cases from 1981,[251] the same court found in two of the cases that rules in Chapters 2 and 8 on how to enact restrictions of basic rights had been respected, but in the third case not. The Supreme Court was more reluctant to exercise judicial review even in cases of that kind,[252] but finally changed its view in a case from 2005,[253] where penal rules in a case concerning legislation on forests were seen to be enacted contrary to Chapter 8, Articles 7 and 13 IG (rules that are extremely technical).

329. Those cases must generally be seen in the light of the general reluctance towards judicial review as a phenomenon that has until recently dominated in Swedish constitutional and political thinking, where it has simply been seen as

248. Conflicts between lower norms and FPA or FSA are of course also theoretically possible, but in reality much less likely to occur, since almost all the cases under those two constitutional acts that come before the court are criminal cases where the system for penal responsibility in the two acts is being examined.
249. Nergelius, *supra*.
250. See not least RÅ 1982 1:74 and more in detail Nergelius, Svensk statsrätt, p. 222 s.
251. RÅ 1981 2:1, 14 and 15.
252. See e.g., NJA 1984, p. 648.
253. NJA 2005, p. 33.

undemocratic and not as a natural part of a living, vital democracy. It is only lately, under the influence of European law, that this opinion has slightly changed. Thus, it is only logical that it is within this area that we find the most interesting judicial review cases from the last few years.

§4. Judicial Review in Relation to European Law

I. Introduction

330. Though the supremacy of European law in general and EU law in particular in relation to Swedish national law should of course have been a clear and generally recognized fact ever since Sweden joined the EU in 1995, it is nevertheless a fact that Swedish courts reacted slowly to the possible implications of European law in Swedish national law, taking much time to fully recognize and acknowledge that accession to the EU meant, among other things, clear limitations for the powers of the sovereign legislator, also in politically highly sensitive matters. This was evident in some cases where the highest courts, the Supreme Court (*Högsta Domstolen*) as well as the Supreme Administrative Court (*Regeringsrätten*) simply made a few clear mistakes by misinterpreting preliminary rulings from ECJ[254] or not asking for such judgments from ECJ in cases where that would have been highly justified and even required.[255] Also an already mentioned, clearly contestable interpretation of the European Convention of Human Rights, contrary to the interpretation made afterwards by the Strasbourg court in a similar case, should be mentioned here.[256]

331. Those issues, and the general attitudes of Swedish courts in view of the new situation in particular, have been heavily debated in Swedish legal doctrine,[257] which has however also observed the 'positive' tendencies, in terms of increased

254. In particular the so-called *Data Delecta* case, NJA (*Nytt Juridiskt Arkiv*) 1996, p. 668. Also the so-called Volvo Service case, NJA 1998, p. 474, where the Supreme Court refused to await the outcome in a similar case pending before the ECJ before rendering its own judgment (and then deciding in favour of Volvo, against the interest of a small car repair service, contrary to the conclusion to which ECJ a few months later arrived in the case C-63/97, *BMW v. Deenik*, ECR 1999 I, p. 905) may be mentioned here.

255. Apart from the Volvo Service case, mentioned in the previous footnote, in particular the rather well-known Barsebäck case concerning the closure of a nuclear reactor comes to mind here; see RÅ (*Regeringsrättens Årsbok*) 1999 ref. 76 (criticized most recently by the former ECJ référendaire Martin Johansson, in Sveinbjörnsdottir confirmed by Högsta Domstolen. But reluctance to apply Community law seems to persist, Europarättslig tidskrift (ERT) 2005, pp. 507–519).

256. NJA 1998, p. 817, concerning the fate of a journalist protesting against Norwegian seal hunting, which ran contrary to the judgment of the European Court of Human Rights in *Bladet Tromsö and Stensaas v. Norway*, 20 May 1999 in case 21980/93, No??

257. In the vast literature on the topic, see e.g., Nergelius, Förvaltningsprocess, normprövning och Europarätt, Stockholm 2000, Ulf Bernitz, Sverige och Europarätten, Stockholm 2002 (also published in English, Sweden and European law) and Iain Cameron, The Swedish Experience of the European Convention of Human Rights since Incorporation, International Comparative Law Quarterly 1999, pp. 20–56. More detailed analysis of case law from Swedish courts in this respect may be found in Kent Karlsson/F. Hägglund, En kartläggning av Sveriges första fem år med EG-rätt, ERT 1999,

judicial review and even a kind of judicial activism, that this 'Europeanization' of Swedish law in the late 1990s brought about.[258] In particular, this has been the case after the important judgments on the prohibition against double sanctions of the supreme court in 2013 mentioned above, but the debate started earlier.To summarize this discussion, I think it is fair to say that the 'sub-ordination', more or less, of Swedish law in some respects to European law represents the most important constitutional change in modern Swedish constitutional history, which has indeed transformed the constitutional perspective also in other ways. Above all, it has meant that above the traditionally so important and very rarely contested legislation, we now in Sweden and some other Nordic countries have not only some rather old and very rarely invoked constitutions, but also the European Convention of Human Rights[259] and the whole body or mass of EU law (*'l'acquis communautaire'*). This has meant, first, that conflicts between the traditionally highly respected and hardly contested laws and norms of a higher dignity have become much more frequent than before and, second, that it is no longer considered as strange to invoke the constitution itself in legal proceedings – a fact that is undoubtedly important at least in Sweden.

332. In the previously mentioned case *Lassagård* from 1997, the plaintiff applied for an agricultural subsidy to a regional administrative authority (*Länsstyrelsen*) in May 1995. The application, based on an EC Regulation, was rejected because the time limit was not respected. Lassagård AB exercised its right to appeal to the superior administrative agency. The agency, however, upheld the previous decision in January 1996. There was no general recourse to judicial review of decisions made by administrative authorities and the review was conditioned by the existence of an explicit statutory provision. Finally, after numerous appeals to different courts, the case reached the Supreme Administrative Court.[260] The main question at issue was to consider whether the lack of judicial review was contrary to

---

pp. 437–519 and in a special addendum to No. 3 of that journal in 1999 (concerning EC law), as well as in J. Södergren, Axplock, ERT 2002, p. 664 ss and 2005, p. 33 ss (concerning ECHR).

258. See e.g., Ola Wiklund, EG-rättens inflytande över svensk rätt – En konstitutionell omvandling, in U. Bernitz/O. Wiklund (eds.), Nordiskt lagstiftningssamarbete i det nya Europa, Stockholm 1996, p. 59 as well as Nergelius, The Impact of EC Law in Swedish National Law – A Cultural Revolution, in I. Cameron/A. Simoni (ed.), Dealing with Integration – Vol. 2, Uppsala 1998, pp. 165–182 and Maktdelning och politikens judikalisering, in SOU 1999:58 (Löser juridiken demokratins problem?), pp. 55–84. Perhaps the clearest expression of an awareness from Swedish courts of the supremacy of EU law is the so-called *Lassagård* case from 1997 (RÅ 1997 ref. 65), where the Supreme Administrative Court set aside a rather crucial law concerning legal remedies in administrative law because it was found to be contrary to the general principles of EU law.

259. During the 1990s, the Convention was incorporated into the national law of all the Nordic states, which was necessary in order to give it a legally binding force in those countries, that are traditionally dualistic in the way they consider the relationship between national and international law. The incorporation was not done at exactly the same time or in exactly the same way in all the five states, but that is a detail that will not be dealt with here.

260. The company appealed to the District Administrative court in Jönköping in May 1996 (the regional agency was located in Jönköping), and the Court considered that the right to a subsidy constituted a civil right in the sense of Art. 6 ECHR. By consequence, Lassagård was entitled to judicial review. However, the competence was not fixed. The Administrative Court of Appeal of Jönköping (August 1996) considered that the absence of judicial review was contrary to Art. 6 ECHR and declared the administrative court to be competent. As to the substance, the Court of Appeal handed the case to the District Administrative Court of Halmstad. (Lassagård was located in Halmstad). The Court

Community law. Interestingly, the issue of Community law was not elucidated by the lower administrative courts that preferred to rely on Article 6 ECHR.

333. The Supreme Administrative Court stressed that no right to judicial review was explicitly provided by Community law, i.e., by the applicable EC regulation. Thus, it was necessary to consider the general principles of Community law enshrined in the jurisprudence of the ECJ. It is worth noting that the general principle that enshrines the right to effective judicial protection results from the *Johnston* case,[261] in which it was stated that the national constitutions and the ECHR (Articles 6 and 13) constituted sources of inspiration regarding the elaboration of the right to effective judicial protection. The national court did however not refer to Johnston but to the *Borelli* case of the ECJ.[262] This case constituted an application of the stare decisis principle, and emphasized that all types of decisions from national authorities regarding individuals' rights stemming from Community law must be subject to judicial review and that Community law prevails over national law. A Community law right was, thus, encroached.[263] Consequently, the Court considered that a court should have jurisdiction to try the case, thereby putting aside the domestic rule, under which there existed no possibility of judicial review. Following the judgment in the *Lassagård* case, the Administrative Procedure Act (*Förvaltningslagen*) was amended in 1998 when an Article 22(a) was incorporated so as to give a general competence to the administrative courts to consider appeals against decisions taken by administrative authorities.

334. The *Lassagård* case is of fundamental importance as to the extension of the scope of judicial review in Sweden and its interaction with European Community law. First, it stems clearly from the case that Community law prevails over domestic law. Second, it may be stated that EC law permits the development of the scope of judicial review in the Swedish legal order. As seen above, the application of the general principle of effective protection by the Supreme administrative Court has resulted in the invalidation of the national regulation limiting review and the simultaneous incorporation of a new provision ensuring the general competence of the administrative courts to review administrative decisions.

335. If any particular decision should be seen as symptomatic or symbolic for the development described here and the rather far-reaching changes that we have seen in the last few years, it was probably the quite bold decision of the Swedish Labour Court (*Arbetsdomstolen*) in April 2005 to ask for a preliminary ruling in a case where the Swedish Constructors Union decided to issue an action of blockade against a Latvian company that was doing construction work in a town outside Stockholm, with lowly-paid Latvian construction workers, and who could not agree with the Union on the terms of the collective agreement that the latter wanted to

declared itself competent but rejected the application since it was lodged too late. Then, Lassagård appealed to the Administrative Court of Gothenburg, who declared itself incompetent.

261. 222/84, ECR 1986, p. 1651.

262. Case C-97/91 *Borelli* [1992] ECR I-6113.

263. Also, the court found the Swedish ordinance incompatible with Art. 6.1 of the ECHR.

sign.[264] Already this contested decision seemed to challenge certain values of Swedish or Nordic collectivism more than most other cases in recent years, since it deals with such a crucial feature of the Swedish welfare state as the power of the trade unions.

336. To start from the beginning, Laval, a Latvian company, sent or posted some thirty workers to Vaxholm in the archipelago east of Stockholm in the spring of 2004, in order to work at a construction site concerning a school. The Swedish Builders Trade Union urged that Laval should adhere to the central or collective labour agreement (*kollektivavtal*) in the building sector, that had been concluded between itself and the Builders employers organization and in which the levels of payment for different jobs are regulated, since Sweden does not have any laws concerning minimum wage.

337. When the parties were not able to agree on this, the union initiated sanctions and a blockade against the school under construction, which was later also supported by the Electricians Union. As a consequence, Laval was prevented from working in Sweden, it lost its contract for this particular site and later went bankrupt. However, before bankruptcy had become a fact, it initiated proceedings before the Labour court, urging that the actions brought by the union(s) should be declared illegal and that it should be awarded financial compensation. The Labour court then asked for a preliminary ruling concerning the compatibility of the actions or sanctions against Laval with EU law (in particular, but not only, in the field of labour law).[265]

338. This is hardly the place to discuss the rather complicated judgment in the *Laval* case in detail.[266] Suffice it to say that ECJ in December 2007 found that the freedom to provide services outweighed the right to initiate sanctions in order to impose the rules in a collective labour agreement on workers posted from another Member State, although the latter could be seen as a part of the human rights included as General Principles of EU law. As the ECJ expressed it, 'Article 3(7) of Directive 96/71 concerning the posting of workers in the framework of the provision of services cannot be interpreted as allowing the host Member State to make the provision of services in its territory conditional on the observance of terms and conditions of employment which go beyond the mandatory rules for minimum protection'.

---

264. Case A 268/04, questions asked 15 Sep. 2005 in the case A 268/04.
265. The Labour court, which started its work already in 1929, is generally seen as a very important part of the allegedly successful 'Swedish model'. It consists of three members each from the Employers organization and the National Union, as well as one professional judge. This somewhat corporative character of the court has been subject to criticism, but the ECtHR in a case 2004 (*Kellermann v. Sweden*, 41579/98, 26 Oct. 2004) with a narrow margin found that the composition of the court met the requirements in Art. 6 ECHR.
266. Case C-341/05, *Laval un Partneri Ltd v. Svenska Byggnadsförbundet and Others*, ECJ 2007 I p. 11767.

339. The Swedish Labour court then eventually, two years later – a delay that must be some kind of record but partly was due to the fact that the court may have wished for legislative changes that would have made its task easier, but never arrived – settled the case, by granting Laval an economic compensation of roughly EUR 55,000, since the actions taken by the unions violated EU law.[267] As well as the judgment from ECJ, also this latter judgment was highly controversial, though of course generally accepted. It may be noted that the current, right-wing government in Sweden has not greeted it with any enthusiasm. Undoubtedly, this is partly because the fear of provoking the powerful trade union remains strong. Meanwhile, the debate concerning judicial review and the role of the courts goes on.[268]

340. Going further, it must be remarked that EC law offers a better protection for basic human rights within Swedish law than the European Convention of Human Rights (ECHR).[269] That conclusion is based on the fact that in the *Lassagård* case the Swedish rules were set aside because they were contrary to Articles 6 and 13 ECHR as part of EC law, as well as to the general principles of EC law, not because ECHR did apply in itself, 'in its own right' so to speak.[270] This also illustrates the somewhat weak or unclear legal position that ECHR has in Swedish law, where, according to IG Chapter 2, Article 19, no act of law or other provision may be adopted which contravenes Sweden's undertakings under the Convention. ECHR as such was then incorporated through an ordinary law (1994:1219). Still, this does not say anything about what would actually happen should a Swedish law after all be contrary to the provision (an issue that is not dealt with in a satisfactory way by the *travaux préparatoires* either).[271]

341. In general, the courts have thus not been wholly unwilling to face up to this new challenge, though some clear errors have been made by different Swedish courts in this respect (not least by the two Supreme Courts), as mentioned above. Still, given the reactions and reflexes also of courts like e.g., the Labour court (*Arbetsdomstolen*), it could in fact be justified to state that the full, total extent of the impact of European law in general and EU law in particular had not really dawned on the Swedish courts during the first then years of EU membership, but that very much has improved since then.[272]

342. A clear sign or indication of this fact also came when the EU Commission in the fall of 2004 addressed the Swedish government with a request for an

267. AD 2009:89.
268. It may be noted here, however, that all seven parties who are members of the Swedish Parliament have agreed to strengthen the courts and widen the scope of judicial review, through a constitutional change that will take effect after the election in September 2010.
269. It may also be said the general principle of effective judicial protection offers a better scope of protection than Arts 6 and 13 ECHR and their corresponding jurisprudence.
270. This question is dealt with further by Nergelius, The Impact of EC Law in Swedish National Law – A Cultural Revolution, in I. Cameron/A. Simoni (ed.), Dealing with Integration (vol. 2) – Perspectives from Seminars on European Law 1996–98, Uppsala 1998, pp. 165–182.
271. For criticism against this fact, see Bernitz, European Law in Sweden, Stockholm 2002, p. 81 ss.
272. *For a comprehensive though critical study*, see *Ulf Bernitz, Förhandsavgöranden av EU-domstolen – Svenska domstolars hållning och praxis, SIEPS 2010:2.*

explanation of the fact that Swedish courts had so rarely, since 1995, asked for preliminary rulings from the ECJ.[273] Having faced this criticism, Sweden decided to enact a new law by the 1 July 2006, which states that if leave for appeal (*prövningstillstånd*) is not granted by any of the two highest courts in cases where matters of EU law are invoked, those two courts have to state the reasons for such an omission or decision.[274] Undoubtedly, also this 'move under pressure' from the Swedish legislator – which proved that previous critics of the exaggerated cautiousness in this respect from the highest courts were not entirely wrong – has contributed to a sharpened and heightened awareness concerning the importance and relevance of European law among Swedish lawyers.

343. Still, it was only in 2005 that the Supreme Court, in particular, showed that it was finally willing to grasp and comply with the full effect not only of the supremacy of EU law, but also of the European Convention of Human Rights. In two judgments during that year (as well as in one request for a preliminary ruling), the Supreme Court arrived at conclusions that may in light of its previous case law in this area only be described as sensational, having used argumentations that were also highly unusual and unexpected in a historical context.

II. Two Unexpected Judgments from 2005

344. The two important judgments that were delivered by the Supreme Court thus both concerned the European Convention of Human Rights, the status of which in Swedish domestic law has in fact been disputed ever since 1 January 1995, when Sweden joined the EU. At the same time, a decision was made by the Swedish Parliament to finally incorporate the ECHR into Swedish national law, which was necessary in order to make it legally binding in Sweden, given the country's traditionally dualistic view on the relationship between international and national law. This was a logical move, given that ECHR is also a part of EU law and that the Convention was already being used by Swedish courts as a means of interpretation,[275] but at the same time it was not done by clearly stating that the Convention was now superior to Swedish law. Instead, as mentioned previously, an Article was

273. The official name or reference of the letter from the Commission is 2003/2161, C (2004) 3899. The cases that led the Commission to initiate this action was partly the above-mentioned *Barsebäck* case (RÅ 1999 ref. 76), which led to a vivid debate, but also the *Lyckeskog* case, C-99/00, ECR I 2002, p. 4839, where the Court of Appeal in Gothenburg asked whether it was to be considered as the highest instance in a petty criminal case. During the proceedings in that case, it seems to have occurred to the EU Commission that when the two highest courts in Sweden decide *not* to grant a leave for appeal, they are not obliged to justify their decisions, which means that they could in fact 'ignore' Art. 234, s. 3 of the EC Treaty without there being any real possibility to control their actions. The Commission, hardly surprising, found this possibility in combination with the generally low frequency of demands for preliminary rulings from Swedish courts unsatisfactory and thus decided to take action against it.

274. The new law is called Lag (2006:502) med vissa bestämmelser om förhandsavgörande från EG-domstolen. It was based on the report Förhandsavgörande från EG-domstolen, Ju2004/9463/DOM.

275. See e.g., the Supreme Court cases NJA 1988, p. 572 and 1991, p. 512 (I).

invoked in Chapter 2 of the IG, according to which laws may not be enacted which are contrary to the Convention. This Article (Chapter 2, Article 19) does however not reveal what would actually happen should a law that is contrary to the European Convention in fact be passed by the Swedish Parliament, which is the result of a legally not so fortunate political compromise from 1993.[276] One of the results of this solution is that a certain basic right is better protected if it may be invoked under EC law than if it is 'only' part of and protected by the ECHR, as shown by the *Lassagård* case from 1997, where the fact that a right to a legal hearing and a fair trial could be deduced not only from ECHR but also from EC law was decisive for the outcome, as seen above.[277]

345. In other words, the ECHR, despite being referred to in IG Chapter 2, Article 19, has not been given constitutional status, but is as such incorporated through an ordinary law.[278] IG 2:19 simply states that 'No act of law or other provision may be adopted' which contravenes Sweden's undertakings under the ECHR. Thus, as mentioned above this may be seen as a rule directed to the legislator rather than the courts.[279]

346. What does this mean in practice, then? It could of course be seen to indicate that when a conflict, which is not manifest, will arise between the ECHR and a Swedish law or ordinance, the law or ordinance shall be applied.[280] But on the other hand, it must be noted that in the *travaux préparatoires*, both from the government and the Constitutional Committee of the Parliament, mention is made of the 'special character' and status of ECHR, which ought to give it a certain weight of its own in future conflicts with domestic laws (or ordinances).[281] On the basis of those remarks, Swedish courts ought to be able to find at least some room for *manoeuvring* if they want to secure the respect (or even supremacy) of the ECHR.

347. Still, which is perhaps not entirely surprising against this background, the Swedish courts have so far been reluctant to use the ECHR, at least when this would mean setting aside a national law. In one case from 1998,[282] the Supreme Court as mentioned above even refused to uphold the Convention (as well as the Freedom of

276. The *travaux préparatoires* where some not so convincing explanations for the compromise sought are presented may be found in SOU 1993:40, prop. 1993/94:117 and the report from the Constitutional Committee of the Parliament (*Konstitutionsutskottet*) 1993/94:24. For critical discussions in the doctrine, see Bernitz, *supra*, Ch. 5 of the book, which is called The Incorporation of the European Human Rights Convention into Swedish Law – A half Measure and Nergelius, Svensk statsrätt, Lund 2014, p. 174 ss.
277. RÅ 1997 ref. 65.
278. The number of which is 1994:1500.
279. Cfr Cameron, An Introduction to the European Convention on Human Rights, 4th ed., Uppsala 2002, p. 155 ss, as well as Bernitz, European Law in Sweden, p. 81 ss.
280. This is the view presented by Cameron, *supra*, p. 159. – Of course, it shall also be noted that the similarities between ECHR and Ch. 2 IG, which contains a rights catalogue, are striking. The main difference is that the protection of personal integrity and family life (Art. 8 ECHR) is definitely weaker in the Swedish constitution(s), given not least the wide right to access to documents in Sweden.
281. Prop 1993/94:117, p. 37 s as well as KU 1993/94:24, p. 19 s.
282. NJA 1998, p. 817.

Speech Act) against a demand from Swedish and Norwegian authorities to execute a penal judgment from a Norwegian court (which was all the more embarrassing since Norway was six months later condemned by EctHR for violating the ECHR concerning the same issue).[283] At the same time, both the highest courts have been very clear in terms of acknowledging e.g., the impact of the principle of proportionality, flowing from ECHR.[284]

348. In the last few years, questions related to administrative tax sanctions (or penalties) and the possibility for Swedish courts to impose damages when the Convention has been violated have been in the focus of the discussion, as mentioned above. In both areas, it seems clear that while EctHR has found that certain violations of ECHR had taken place in Sweden, Swedish courts were slow or even reluctant to take the full consequences of those judgments and come to the same conclusions as the EctHR did in almost identical cases.[285] As far as economic compensation for violations of the convention is concerned, Swedish courts tended to view this as an exclusive competence of the EctHR, though this was not quite in line with the case law of that court, nor with ECHR itself (see not least its Article 13).

349. The importance of the so-called *Lundgren* case, NJA 2005, p. 462, should thus be seen in this light. In that case, which must be seen as a breakthrough for the direct applicability of the ECHR in Swedish law, a man had been informed that he was suspected of economic crimes in 1991. Since then, he had difficulties supporting himself; his company went bankrupt and after that it was hard for him to find any other job. A criminal charge was raised against him in 1993, but the trial did not take place until 1997 and the acquitting sentence from the Court of First Instance did not win its full legal force and effect (*laga kraft*) before the fall of 1998. This time-extension of the procedure was considered as unacceptable and contrary to Article 6 of ECHR by the Supreme Court, which granted Lundgren, the formerly accused man who was now the claimant in the tort case, financial compensation due

---

283. *Bladet Tromsö and Stensaas v. Norway*, case 21980/93, Reports 1999 p. The case concerned Norwegian fishermen who had publicly criticized methods used in the hunting of seal. For this, they were condemned to penalties by Norwegian courts, which in the case before EctHR was considered to be a violation of their freedom of speech (Art. 10 ECHR). The Swedish case concerned a fisher, Odd Lindberg, who had made such critical comments in a TV program which was later broadcasted in Sweden (and thus also seen in Norway, where almost everyone is able to watch Swedish TV). He was therefore also sentenced to a fine by a Norwegian court. The Norwegian authorities then chased him, after he had taken refuge to Sweden, eager to have the penalty imposed. They were then helped by the Swedish authorities and the Supreme Court could not find that the ECHR prevented those from executing the fine in Sweden (despite the fact that under the Freedom of Speech Act, the editor of the TV program and not Lindberg himself was legally responsible for any comments made in the program). From at least two points of view (and maybe also considering so-called *ordre public* in private international law), therefore, this judgment must be considered as a clear error.
284. See e.g., besides the cases referred to above in fn. 47, the case NJA 2001, p. 439.
285. The procedure for imposing administrative tax sanctions (skattetillägg) has for example been found by EctHR to be contrary to Art. 6 ECHR in the Cases *Janosevic and Västberga Taxi/Vulic v. Sweden*, 34619 and 36985/97, judgment 23 Jul. 2002, Reports 2002 p.

to the fact that Swedish public authorities had not complied with the ECHR. As indicated above, the judgment followed after some previous cases where lower courts had totally refused to grant financial compensation due to the fact that the ECHR had been violated by public authorities. Still, the Supreme Court in 2003, in the so-called *Holm* case,[286] had indicated that such financial compensation could after all occur, had the Convention really been violated, which was thus found to be the case here, two years later. Lundgren was consequently awarded compensation from the state first for his financial losses, based on his loss of income during a number of years, formally according to the rules in the Swedish Tort law (*Skadeståndslagen*) but in reality because Swedish authorities had violated Article 6 of ECHR, with the sum of SEK 700,000. On top of that, he was also granted compensation for that violation as such, in itself so to speak (so-called *ideell skada* or immaterial damage) with SEK 100,000. In that latter respect, the right to compensation, interestingly enough, was considered as a part of the obligation that Sweden owns within its national law, according to Article 13 of ECHR, to provide efficient remedies in order to prevent or compensate violations of the Convention within due time. This jurisprudence has been reinforced in subsequent case law in 2012[287] and, as mentioned above, in 2014 also with respect to the catalogue of rights in Chapter 2 IG.[288]

350. One effect of the judgment is, in my view, that Article 13 of ECHR may now be considered as a general rule on financial compensation, which is henceforth to be applied by national courts when it has been clearly established that violations of the Convention have really taken place. So far, there has been fairly little debate in the Swedish doctrine concerning the implications of the judgment,[289] but such a conclusion can hardly be too far-reaching. Apart from that, it seems likely that the judgment will have far-reaching implications also concerning future situations where individuals rightly or wrongly feel that they have been badly treated by public authorities. The judgment in the *Lundgren* case is therefore likely to increase the rule of law and the legal certainty in Sweden in the future, hopefully also in cases where the claimant argues that the IG or some other constitutional act has been violated.

351. The circumstances in the other remarkable case from 2005, the internationally well-known and observed *Reverend Åke Green* case, which has merited considerable attention worldwide, were perhaps even more peculiar. As may be well-known to the reader, the case concerned a reverend (not in the official, formerly state church (*Svenska kyrkan*) but in a smaller religious community), who during a sermon in July 2003 made an unprecedented, unexpected and very brutal or even violent attack against homosexuals as a group. Quoting and referring to the bible he

286. NJA 2003, p. 217.
287. NJA 2012 p. 211 (I-II).
288. NJA 2014 pp. 323 and 332.
289. See however Åhman in Juridisk Tidskrift (JT) 2005/06, pp. 424–430, as well as Södergren in that same journal 2004/05, pp. 762–775.

warned, among other things, against an increased spread of aids through legalization of homosexual relations, called the legislators who had made such official relations possible and legal 'lunatics' and denounced homosexuals as a 'cancer tumour' in the societal body. He also made it clear that he had been in touch with media before the speech and had actually been active in trying to spread his views in the general debate; consequently, newspapers and a local TV station were invited to his sermon.

352. The Swedish law on agitation or incitement against certain minorities or groups of people (*hets mot folkgrupp*) had actually been amended only a few years before, in order to include also incitement against persons which is based on their sexual orientation. Thus, it was fairly clear that Reverend Green had in fact violated this Swedish law and he was also sentenced for this (to one month in prison) by the city court in Kalmar in south-east Sweden. Still, the question was of course if this Swedish law was compatible with the Swedish constitution and the European Convention of Human Rights, which do both protect freedom of speech as well as freedom of religion. The Court of Appeal did not think so and found that in particular the freedom of religion, given that the remarks were made during a sermon, outweighed the Swedish legislation (given also that according to the Swedish Constitution, IG Chapter 2, Articles 1, 23 and 24, the freedom of religion is as such unrestricted and not possible to limit by law).

353. The state prosecutor (*Riksåklagaren*) who has an unlimited right to bring cases to the Supreme Court, appealed against this acquitting sentence and claimed that Green should be sentenced to a prison punishment. The argumentation of the Supreme Court in this case was particularly interesting – and at the same time slightly puzzling and confusing – in a European law perspective.

354. The Supreme Court analysed the new Swedish legislation in some detail and first of all, quite surprisingly or at least unexpectedly rapidly, came to the conclusion that it was not contrary to the protection of freedom of speech and religion in the Swedish constitution. This was done by invoking the requirement of manifest error in IG Chapter 11, Article 14, which may have been right or wrong in this case but was here definitely not done in a very convincing way. Above all, it shall be noted that this restriction on judicial review by the courts applies also in relation to the European Convention on Human Rights, according to IG Chapter 2, Article 19 and its *travaux préparatoires*.[290] Thus, once the Supreme Court had come to that conclusion, it should in fact have been impossible also to claim that the Swedish law was incompatible with ECHR and, consequently, that Green should be acquitted.

355. Nevertheless, the Supreme Court managed to arrive at exactly that result, using a quite complicated line of reasoning according to which the case law of the Strasbourg court clearly shows that the only kind of speech in religious situations

290. But not in relation to EU law, for obvious reasons, as shown e.g., by the *Lassagård* case (RÅ 1997 ref. 65).

which is not protected by the freedoms of religion and speech in Articles 9–10 of the Convention is so-called 'hate speech' or, in other words, clear incitements to violent acts or persecution of specific groups of individuals. Once again, this conclusion may be right or wrong as such,[291] but in this specific case, it led to some quite strange and puzzling results.

356. First of all, the Supreme Court here showed a clear reluctance to really exercise judicial review as such and really decide whether the law in question was after all incompatible with ECHR. Instead, it said that if Green would be sentenced and he would then bring the case to the Strasbourg court – which he had in fact publicly declared that he was in that case going to do – it would be likely that the European Court of Human Rights would find that Sweden had violated the ECHR. But as everyone can see, this is actually less of a judgment based on the existing legal rules that the Supreme Court has to apply than a speculation about the future outcome, should a certain individual decide to act in a certain way and should, then, certain judges in Strasbourg decide to settle the case in a certain manner, in some four or five years from now (given the heavy workload of the Strasbourg court). This attitude may of course be seen as very pro-European indeed, but at the same time the Supreme Court may here be criticized for not exercising its true competence to decide a case and, in fact, even for abdicating from its position as the highest court of the country (and conveniently, in a very controversial case, more or less handling over that role to the Strasbourg court).

357. What actually seems to have been the crucial issue, from the point of view of the Swedish Supreme Court, is to be able to avoid applying the Swedish law without really stating that it is contrary to the ECHR as such, which explains the emphasis and detailed analysis of the jurisprudence of the Strasbourg court in the judgment. Referring to that jurisprudence, the Supreme Court found that it would be impossible to sentence Reverend Green to a punishment, though the new law is still not considered as incompatible with the Convention. Thus, the judgment may be seen as 'pro-European' while still expressing a traditional, cautious attitude to the exercise of judicial review.[292] Time will tell whether it will in the future be considered as a wise and bold judgment or not, but there is no doubt that it reveals a very clear – perhaps even too big – respect from the Supreme Court in relation to the European Court of Human Rights.[293]

358. On top of those two judgments, we may then also mention a third interesting case from 2005, where the Supreme Court contrary to its previous positions and

291. It was in fact based on a heavy amount of quoted case law, including many old and new cases falling under both those two Articles, which must as such be described as solid.

292. In this latter respect, it is similar to yet another – strictly national – case on judicial review from 2005, NJA 2005, p. 33.

293. Apart from that, it also seems clear that it puts opinions made during the exercise of religious activities in a somewhat 'preferred position' in relation to other, similar verbal attacks, a fact that became even clearer when the Supreme Court in 2006 came to a totally different conclusion in a similar case where some neo-nazis who had attacked homosexuals in leaflets, using in fact less provocative words than Reverend Green, were found guilty; see NJA 2006, s. 467.

not too few plain errors in its handling of EU law asked, quite surprisingly, for a preliminary ruling, namely the already mentioned so-called *Unibet* case.[294] That request was highly surprising, since it is an established fact within Swedish law that no right to an *abstract* judicial review exists, as mentioned above;[295] in other words, the courts will only exercise judicial review – under or within the restrictions imposed by IG Chapter 11, Article 14 – when there is a concrete case or dispute pending where the law or legal act in question may be applied and not ever *in abstracto*, just because a certain party may believe for one reason or another that a certain legal act is unconstitutional.[296] Against that background, it was highly surprising when the Supreme Court in November 2005 decided to ask the ECJ if this lack of possibilities in the exercise of judicial review or rather, this limitation of the possible ways under which judicial review may be exercised by Swedish courts, was compatible or not with EU law.[297]

359. If you consider the circumstances of the case, the request is even more surprising, in particular given that ECJ has in fact never demanded any specific details or specific design of any particular model of judicial review within the legal systems of the Member States, as long as a right to an effective remedy may be said to exist (also as far as review of the relationship between EU law and national law is concerned). In this particular case, the gambling company Unibet had been charged by a Swedish prosecutor for violating Swedish gambling and lottery rules. Thus, a criminal case was pending in which Unibet was free to invoke an alleged unconstitutionality or incompatibility with EU law of the Swedish legislation. At the same time, Unibet had sued the Swedish state and asked for financial compensation due to the fact that the company could not freely exercise its trade. And if that was not enough, Unibet had also initiated an administrative procedure in which it was complaining or appealing against not being granted a certain gambling licence. Also in both those two latter proceedings, Unibet was free to invoke any legal arguments it wished, urging the courts to exercise judicial review included.[298] Thus, the likeliness that the ECJ should find that Swedish law is on this particular point contrary to EU law seemed limited, to put it mildly, and the judgment confirmed this by emphasizing that the ECJ leaves it to the Member States to design particularities in the Court system, as long as a right to an effective remedy exists.

294. The case in question, C-432/05, *ECR 2007 I p. 2271*, was decided by the ECJ 13 Mar. 2007, as mentioned above.
295. See in particular NJA 1987 p. 198, where this was clearly declared by the Supreme Court. See also RÅ 1994 n. 277 and 654.
296. I do here, in order to simplify, not deal with certain special features of IG Ch. 11, Art. 14, like the fact that not only courts but also other public authorities may exercise judicial review and that such review may also concern the compatibility of a regulation or decree with a superior rule.
297. The request in question was made in the case(s) Ö-4474-04 and 752-05.
298. In fact, the case which did reach the Supreme Court, and finally the ECJ, was a spin-off effect of one of those procedures, in which Unibet claimed that it had the right to have judicial review exercised independently of the specific dispute taking place before the court. When the Court of First Instance rejected that claim, Unibet appealed both to the Court of Appeal and later to the Supreme Court, that took an unexpected interest in the arguments raised by the company.

360. The cautious attitude of the Supreme Court when asking for the opinion of the ECJ in this case definitely stands in strong contrast to the attitude(s) previously shown by that court in those kind of cases. It is thus yet another example of a change in the positions recently taken by Swedish courts in relation to European law, the reasons of which we must now analyse a little bit more.

III. Conclusions and a View to the Future

361. There is in my view no doubt that the case law from the Swedish Supreme Court presented and analysed above does indeed represent a true shift in the positions taken by the highest Swedish judicial body in relation to European law, in particular when compared to the attitude showed before by that particular court (and partly also by the Supreme Administrative Court). The two judgments are thus important and significant, in many different ways.

362. At the same time, the question may be raised if they – and also the preliminary ruling requested by the Supreme Court in the *Unibet* case – do really represent a true, sincere wish from the Supreme Court to deal with European law in a serious way, or if they are rather to be seen as a step back under pressure, under the gun so to speak – given that the EU Commission had in 2004 protested against a limited use of the instrument of preliminary ruling by Swedish courts (and by the two highest courts in particular) and that there existed by this time a number of voices in the Swedish doctrine that raised criticisms against parts of the jurisprudence from those two courts. Thus, though highly interesting, those two important judgments and the surprising request for a preliminary ruling concerning a very peculiar constitutional matter, are after all not entirely convincing in the sudden pro-European convictions that they reveal. Further substantive proof of a true change of mind from the high Swedish judges is wanted and indeed wished for in this respect, also in cases that do not involve European law so clearly, in order for the critical parts of the doctrine to believe that this sudden reversal of opinion is really to be taken seriously.

363. However, in 2013 the Supreme Court really had to acknowledge the supremacy of European law in relation to Swedish legislation, in the so-called ne bis in idem cases mentioned above.[299] Having for a long time refused to set aside Swedish legislation imposing administrative tax sanctions and criminal sanctions for the same action[300] and also refused, by three votes to two, to ask for a preliminary ruling from the ECJ, as a result of the judgment in the *Åkerberg Fransson* case in February 2013[301] (where a preliminary ruling had been requested by a local court in the north of Sweden), the Supreme Court in a plenary judgment reversed its position and admitted that the system violated the ECHR as well as the EU Charter on Fundamental Rights. After that judgment, it is true to say that a profound change has taken place here.

299. NJA 2013 p. 502 and 746.
300. NJA 2010 p. 168.
301. C-617/10, Judgment of 26 Feb. 2013.

Part V. Specific Problems

§1. War Powers

364. Chapter 15 of IG has the title 'War and danger of war'. It has, fortunately, never been applied and it is thus impossible to know whether or not its rules are well-suited for their purposes.

365. According to Chapter 15, Article 1 the Government or the Speaker shall convene the Parliament in session whenever the Realm finds itself at war or before the danger of war. Such a session must not necessarily be held in Stockholm. Should it be necessary, a so-called War Delegation shall be appointed from the MP's in order to replace the Parliament (IG Chapter 15, Article 2, see also the Riksdag Act Chapter 8, Article 15). The Speaker shall then preside over the 50 MP's of which the Delegation consists. The War Delegation will have the same powers as the Riksdag normally has and may for example decide to amend the Constitution, but it may not decide that new parliamentary elections are going to be held (Chapter 15, Articles 3 and 12).[302] It may thus, as may the Parliament if it is still acting, decide on the formation of a government and determine its working procedure (Chapter 15, Article 4), which will facilitate the formation of a so-called government in exile, should that be necessary.

366. Should however, in case of war, neither the Parliament nor the War Delegation be in a position to carry out its duties, the Government shall assume their respective powers to the extent that it considers necessary to protect the Realm and bring hostilities to a close (Chapter 15, Article 5). It may however never enact, amend or abrogate a constitutional act or the Riksdag Act or the law on Parliamentary elections (*Vallagen*). In other areas of legislation, however, the competence of the Government is heavily increased[303] in times of war or danger of war, as follows from Chapter 15, Article 6, which depends of course on the fact that the Parliament may then not always be able to (re)act as quickly as necessary. For similar reasons, the special provision in Chapter 2, Article 22, section 1 IG according to which certain law proposals may be held in abeyance for a year will not apply during times of war under Chapter 15, Article 7. It is also logical that the Government may,

302. In other words, only the Parliament may decide this. The Parliament may under Ch. 13, Art. 12 also, with a three-fourths majority of the MP's decide to defer previously scheduled elections with one year.
303. Compared to what does otherwise apply according to Ch. 8 IG, that is.

according to Chapter 15, Article 9 IG conclude a ceasefire agreement without seeking the approval of the Parliament and without consulting the special Advisory Council on Foreign Affairs, which follows from Chapter 15, Article 9 IG. An approval would then have to be sought afterwards in accordance with Chapter 10 IG, but surprisingly enough it appears to be a totally open question what should happen if the agreement will not then be approved by the Parliament.

367. Finally, it is regulated in Chapter 15, Article 9 that neither the Parliament nor the Government may make decisions on occupied territory. It should also be noted that powers vested in a person in his capacity as an MP or as a minister may never be exercised on such territory, where elections may never be held and all public authorities are to act in the manner that best serves the defence effort and resistance activities, as well as the protection of the civilian population and Swedish interests at large. Furthermore, public authorities may never make any decisions or take any action which, contrary to international law will impose on a citizen of the Realm the duty of rendering assistance to the occupying power.[304]

368. Concerning the armed forces, the Government may commit them at any time to battle in order to repel an armed attack against the Realm. In other cases, however, a state of war may not be declared without the consent of the Parliament.[305] Those forces may otherwise be committed to battle or dispatched abroad under certain conditions, all of which are laid down in Chapter 15, Article 13 IG; thus, the Parliament must give its consent, the action must be permitted under an act of law which regulates the conditions for the action and a duty to take such action must follow from an international agreement or obligation which has previously been approved by the Parliament. These kind of international commitments are now becoming increasingly important, in Sweden like in many other states.

§2. Emergency Laws

369. The general conception in Swedish constitutional doctrine seems to be that Sweden does not recognize emergency laws as an autonomous source of rules, with constitutional status, since decisions are always made within the frames of IG, whose Chapter 15 will apply in times of war or danger of war.[306] Pure experience, visible for any student of public affairs, does however reveal that this assumption is simply not correct.

304. Those rules were severely sharpened in 1988, after lots of criticism had been directed towards older, leaner rules. Although such rules are of limited value when it comes to protecting the country from occupation, they may be important afterwards, if it will be necessary to decide if certain bodies have acted correctly.
305. See Ch. 10, Art. 9 IG. Under its s. 3, the Government may however at any time authorize the armed forces to use force in accordance with international law in order to prevent violation of Swedish territory.
306. See e.g., Holmberg/Stjernquist, *supra*, p. 236, as well as Algotsson, *supra*, p. 325 ss. The view is however criticized by Nergelius, *supra*, p. 313 s.

370. Most recently, the discussion on emergency laws has been vivid in the aftermath of the tsunami crisis, although the criticism directed against the Government after that has above all concerned its lack of action, instead of it having done too much too fast or in the wrong manner. In other words, the Government was here criticized for failing to understand and recognize the presence of a clear emergency situation. A typical case is otherwise that a minister will refer to the presence of an emergency situation in order to justify actions that would normally have been illegal, because they would have violated for example Chapter 7, Article 2 or Chapter 12, Article 2 IG. For certain reasons, however, that kind of reasoning seems to be more frequent in other Nordic states than in Sweden, which probably has historical reasons.

371. This phenomenon has however occurred in Sweden too, in relation not least to some violent acts that took place in the 1970s (the hi-jacking of an airplane in 1972, a hostage situation in a bank in Stockholm in 1973[307] and not least the occupation of the West German Embassy in Stockholm in 1975) which all led to negotiations between perpetrators and ministers, payments, deportations of suspected criminals who were in a critical state and similar, somewhat problematic actions. Those situations occurred both before and after the enactment of the IG and it is worth noting that the Constitutional Committee has always accepted those explanations from the responsible ministers, specifically because real emergency situations had actually existed.[308] On the other hand, in situations where ministers – and other persons involved in illegal actions – have used the argument in order to justify their actions but no real emergency seems to have occurred, this line of defence has not been accepted, which was clearly seen after the Ebbe Carlsson-scandal in 1988.[309] Having this in mind, it may after all be stated that emergency law is acknowledged as a fact in Sweden, though it may definitely not be regularly invoked or applied.

§3. The Constitutional Relationship between Church and State

372. The new regulation of the Church of Sweden and its implications have been mentioned above in Part I, Chapter 3 and it is therefore not necessary to dwell further on the subject here. The only thing that may be noticed since it may seem to be slightly strange, if Sweden is now supposed to be religiously neutral, is that the Church of Sweden is at all mentioned in Chapter 8, Article 6 IG. This is actually not logical in the new situation and thus hard to explain.[310]

---

307. Which incidentally gave birth to the internationally acknowledged so-called 'Stockholm syndrome', i.e., the situation when the hostage(s) tend to sympatize more with the perpetrators than with the surrounding police forces.
308. See e.g., KU 1974:22, p. 19 ss and 1975/76:50, p. 34 ss.
309. See above in Part II, Chapter?? and KU 1988/89:30.
310. Cfr Algotsson, Sveriges författning efter EU-anslutningen, p. 226 s.

Selected Bibliography

Algotsson, K.-G.: Sveriges författning efter EU-anslutningen, Stockholm 2000 (SNS).

Bernitz, U. *Sweden and European Law*, Stockholm: Juristförlaget, 2002 – Europarättens Genomslag, Stockholm, 2012.

Bull, T./F. Sterzel. Regeringsformen – En Kommentar, 2nd ed., Lund, 2013.

Eka, A./Hirschfeldt, J./Jermsten, H./Svahn Starrsjö, K. Regeringsformen – Med Kommentarer. Stockholm, 2012.

Groussot, X. General Principles of Community Law, Groningen 2006 (European Law Papers), Chapter 9.

Holmberg, E./Stjernquist, N./Isberg, M./Eliason, M./Regner, G.: Grundlagarna – Regeringsformen, Successionsordningen, Riksdagsordningen, 2nd ed., Stockholm (Norstedts) 2006.

Modéer, Kjell Å. Wissenschaft vom Verfassungsrecht: Schweden, in A. von Bogdandy/P. Cruz Villalon/P. Huber (eds.), Handbuch Ius Publicum Europaeum, Band II – Offene Staatlichleit. Wissenschaft vom Verfassungsrecht, Heidelberg 2007 pp. 697–713.

Nergelius, J.: Svensk statsrätt, Lund (Studentlitteratur) 3rd ed. 2014 – The Influence of EU Membership on Swedish Law, in P. Luif (ed.), Österreich, Schweden, Finnland – Zehn Jahre Mitgliedschaft in der Europäischen Union, 3rd ed., Vienna (Böhlau) 2007, pp. 131–143.

Sweden's Possible Ratification of the EU Constitution: A Case-study of 'Wait and See'. In *The EU Constitution and National Constitutions: Ratification and Beyond*, edited by A. Albi/J. Ziller. The Hague, 2006, pp. 183–188.

Reasons Why a Small Country Would Want to Become a Member of the European Union (Taking the Nordic Countries as Examples), in European Integration: History and Perspectives, vol. 45. Lausanne: Institut Suisse de Droit Comparé, 2002, pp. 65–76.

Constitutional Law. In *Swedish Legal System*, edited by M. Bogdan. Stockholm: Norstedts, 2010, pp. 39–65.

Offene Staatlichkeit. Schweden, in A. von Bogdandy/P. Cruz Villalon/P. Huber (eds.), Handbuch Ius Publicum Europaeum, Band II – Offene Staatlichleit. Wissenschaft vom Verfassungsrecht, Heidelberg 2007 pp. 277–311.

Scandinavian Studies in Law, vol. 52, Stockholm 2007, is a special edition entirely devoted to Constitutional Law.

Warnling-Nerep, W.: En orientering i tryckfrihet och yttrandefrihet, 3rd ed., Stockholm 2005.

Warnling-Nerep, W./Lagerqvist Veloz Roca, A./Reichel, J.: Statsrättens grunder, Stockholm (Norstedts), 2005 (2nd ed. 2007).

Selected Bibliography

Åhman, Karin: Normprövning – Domstols kontroll av svensk lags förenlighet med Regeringsformen och Europarätten 2000–2010.

The four constitutional Acts as well as the Parliamentary Act are translated into English and edited by the Swedish Parliament in the volume The Constitution of Sweden – The Fundamental Laws and the Riksdag Act, Stockholm 2012 (where the term Constitution, for IG and the other single acts, is replaced by Fundamental Law).[311]

311. That official translation is being used throughout this book, when different sections of the Swedish constitutional acts are referred to *or quoted*. Thus, the responsible part for any errors of translation is in fact the Swedish Parliament.

Index

The numbers here refer to paragraph numbers.

Abstract judicial review, 322, 358
Accession to European Union, 12, 330
Access to documents, 6, 275, 295, 299, 310
Acclamation (voting rule), 178
Acquis communautaire, 154, 331
Administrative decisions, 334
Anti-terrorism measures, 280
Armed forces, 368
Autonomous competence (government), 41
Autonomy of public administration, 222

Bicameral Parliament of, 8, 10
Budget (budgetary) regulations, 111

Chamber of Parliament, 206
Charges, 40, 223, 349
Church of Sweden, 33, 372
Civil servants, 69, 201, 205, 224
Constituencies, 55, 96
Constitutional changes amendments, 23, 29, 30, 206
Constitutional custom, 46
Constitution, normative force of, 46
Contributions to political parties, 60
Convergence criteria, 156
Corruption, 11, 57, 64, 77, 233, 295
Council of State, meeting of, 83
Court system organization of, 237

Declaration of no-confidence, 191
Decrees, 34–44, 107
Delegation of legislative powers, 38, 107, 110, 120
Déni de justice, 247
Deputy Prime Minister, 182, 196
Deputy Speakers, 100, 185, 189
Discharge of minister, 180, 189–191
Dualism, 21, 255, 344

Economic and Monetary Union (EMU), 122, 130, 131, 154–159
Electoral campaigns, 71
Electoral law, 57, 60, 73, 94
Equality before the law, 18, 45
Equality between men and women, 87, 241
EU Constitution, 152, 161, 164, 165
EU-nämnden, 153
European Convention of Human Rights (ECHR), 2, 15, 22, 237, 240, 254–260, 262, 264, 265, 268–270, 272, 278, 282, 314, 327, 328, 330–333, 340, 343–350, 352, 354, 356, 357, 363
European Union general, 330, 341
European Union transfer of powers to, 152
Exchange Rate Mechanism, 157
Exile government, 365
Extraordinary elections, 53, 97, 98, 188, 191, 208

Favourable provisions, 42
Financial compensation, 281, 285, 294, 337, 349, 350, 359
Finansutskottet, 116, 173
Foreigners rights of, 272, 286
Freedom of assembly, 274, 276, 291
Freedom of association, 277, 278, 291
Freedom of information, 275, 299
Freedom of movement, 281
Freedom of Press Act of (FPA), 1, 6, 9, 15, 25, 254, 274, 275, 295–307
Freedom of religion, 90, 270, 277, 352
Freedom of speech, 15, 25, 69, 254, 274, 275, 295, 296, 305, 352, 354
Freedom to demonstrate, 276

General Principles of Law, 45

Index

Governmental bills (propositioner), 47, 170, 171
Government appointment of, 8, 180, 305
Government collective responsibility of, 54, 181, 198, 200
Government dischargement of, 54, 180, 192
Government office, 194, 231
Grundlagsutredningen, 20, 138, 206, 214

Hierarchy of norms, 19, 20, 107

Immunity for MP's, 105
Implementation of laws, 41
Incorporation, 12, 255–257, 334
Individual initiatives of MP's, 170
Instrument of Government of, 1, 2, 4, 6, 7, 15, 16, 20, 25, 48, 89, 107–119, 134–153, 270–294, 319
International agreements, 23, 24, 134, 152, 368
Interpellation questions, 204
Interpretation methods, 247

Judges, appointment and removal of, 239, 240
Judges, salaries to, 238, 240
Judicial activism, 331
Judicial independence, 235
Judicial review, 19, 44, 147, 221, 254–363
Judicial self-restraint, 318
Jury system, 297, 304
Justitiekanslern, 229
Justitieombudsman, 197, 229

King penal immunity of, 85
Konstitutionsutskottet, 27, 173
Konungabalken, 3

Law Council (lagrådet), 171
Laws, 6, 20, 25, 27, 34, 39, 41, 45, 47, 107, 109, 226, 246, 255, 258, 269, 281, 288, 311, 314, 315, 317, 324, 325, 328, 331, 336, 344, 346, 369–371
Leave for appeal, 342
Legal effects of criminal acts, 37
Legislation, 8, 23, 31–33, 35, 46, 47, 62, 71, 107–110, 115, 163, 169–178, 194, 235, 264, 265, 272, 280, 282, 310, 315, 316, 328, 331, 352, 354, 359, 363, 366

Lex superior, 20
Liability rules, 301
Lobbyists, 74
Local self-government, 16, 243

Ministers responsibility of, 197, 225
Ministries, 180, 194, 203
Minority governments, 57, 119, 174, 184
Muhammed crisis, 217
Municipal autonomy, 245, 246
Municipal elections, 49
Municipal taxes, 112

National Audit Office (Riksrevisionen), 212, 214, 229
National Bank (Riksbank), 111, 159, 229
National elections, 14, 49, 91, 92, 103, 249
Negative parliamentarianism, 179, 183, 187, 221

Objectivity and impartiality, 18
One-chamber Parliament, 10, 14
Ordinary elections, 53, 97–99, 188, 189, 191

Parliamentary committees, 20, 27, 116, 118, 153, 170, 173, 205, 210, 225, 233, 310
Parliamentary compromises, 174
Parliamentary control, 204, 207, 220
Parliamentary debate, 102, 155
Parliamentary session, 100, 171, 172
Party groups, 53, 185, 189
Personal liberty, 281
Political accountability, 203, 215, 221
Political advisors, 226
Popular sovereignty, 10, 13, 16, 20, 26, 31, 48, 119, 220, 227, 309, 324
Preliminary rulings, 266, 267, 330, 335, 337, 342, 343, 358, 362, 363
Prime minister, 14, 20, 50, 53, 54, 84, 100, 155, 180–183, 185–192, 195, 196, 198, 208, 209, 215–217, 221, 223, 234, 318–326
Prior scrutiny, 307
Procedural guarantees, 272, 282
Proportional election system, 56
Proportionality principle, 45, 259, 347
Protection of basic rights, 143, 147

Referendum, 28, 29, 52, 78–79, 110, 121, 122, 127, 130, 132, 139, 143, 145, 154, 155, 158, 160, 165, 167, 168
Regional autonomy, 244, 245, 251
Regionalization, 242, 245, 250, 253
Regulations, 9, 34–45, 77, 107, 108, 111, 118, 134, 146, 153, 160, 179, 180, 272, 276, 278, 295, 324, 327, 332–334, 372
Requirement of manifest error, 318, 319, 324, 326, 354
Restrictions of basic rights, 328
Right to property, 270, 272, 283, 284, 294
Riksåklagaren, 353
Riksdag Act, 9, 25, 32, 83, 99–101, 107, 109, 116, 118, 134, 153, 171–176, 178, 189, 204, 205, 310, 365, 366
Royal family religion of, 90
Rule of law, 13, 48, 163, 235, 272, 282, 311, 315, 350

Separation of powers, 10, 13, 26, 48, 206, 235, 242
Social economic and cultural rights, 16
Speaker of Parliament, 53, 185
State aid to political parties, 65, 68
Sub-delegation, 108
Succession to throne, 1, 9, 15, 25, 82, 87, 88
Supremacy of EU law, 162, 343

Taxes (taxation), 17, 37, 40, 110–113, 173, 243, 246–248, 264, 310
Transparency in public administration, 11, 201
Travaux préparatoires, 47, 148, 151, 257, 258, 314, 319, 340, 346, 354
Tsunami disaster, 84

Utrikesnämnden, 83

Vote of no-confidence, 191, 200

War Delegation, 365, 366
Whistleblowers, 293, 299

Index